Geordies
Roots of Regionalism

Edited by Robert Colls and Bill Lancaster

Geordies is an affectionate but realistic portrait of the North-East of England, past, present and future. Banishing stereotypes, it describes this distinctive region's origins and development, advocating the German *Bundesländer* system to promote economic renewal.

Drawing on history, geography, political economy, popular culture, music, literature and sport, *Geordies* celebrates the history and culture of the North-East. It highlights a region with exemplary racial integration, as well as a city with a thriving artistic centre, excellent amenities and renowned sense of humour. Geordies have always known how to have a good time, and famous exports include the Pet Shop Boys, Gaza and *Viz*, not to mention Emily Davison and Brian Redhead. This book shows why the North-East is firmly in the public mind, laying as much claim to regional, political and cultural identity within the new Europe as, for example, Catalonia, Brittany or Bavaria.

ROBERT COLLS was born in South Shields and now teaches History at Leicester University. He has written several books, including *The Pitmen of the Northern Coalfield*.

BILL LANCASTER was born in Blaydon and is now Senior Lecturer in History at the University of Northumbria at Newcastle. He is author of *Radicalism, Co-operation and Socialism* and co-author with Tony Mason of *Life and Labour in a 20th-century City*.

Geordies
Roots of Regionalism

Edited by
ROBERT COLLS
and
BILL LANCASTER

EDINBURGH UNIVERSITY PRESS

© Edinburgh University Press, 1992

Edinburgh University Press
22 George Square, Edinburgh

Typeset in Linotron Baskerville
by Redwood Typesetting Ltd, and
printed in Great Britain by
Redwood Press Ltd, Melksham

A CIP record for this book is available
from the British Library

ISBN o 7486 0394 8

In
MEMORY
of
JACK COMMON and SID CHAPLIN
and
FOR
THE PEOPLE OF THE NORTH-EAST

Contents

—

CONTENTS

Preface

———

THIS BOOK IS BY GEORDIES, about Geordies, and we take as our place the whole North-East region. For now, this means the old counties of Northumberland and Durham, but it is possible to envisage circumstances when it could be taken to mean more. Over seventy years ago, the geographer Fawcett called for 'A North Country', extending out of the two counties to include Teesside and part of the North Riding, and through the Tyne Gap to include most of Cumberland and north Westmorland.[1] Events did not match Fawcett's hopes, but, like him, we believe there is nothing sacrosanct in borders. Whether the North-East region ever *could* be taken to mean more will depend upon the interplay of twenty-first-century politics and economics. We will have to wait and see how far Geordies can reach.

Just to include Northumberland and Durham as 'Geordie' will offend some people. No offence is intended. We do not wish to be dogmatic about what is heartfelt. In any case, there is clearly nothing that a little book like this will do to shift the ingrained loyalties of county patriots. Nor does it wish to. Those 'real' Northumbrians for instance, who see themselves as the inheritors of eleventh-century Boernican kingdoms, are not likely to be much fussed by yet another level of identity overlaying all the other levels which have been and gone since 1018. Old invented traditions are always fusing with new invented traditions, and nowhere more so than in the case of people's identities. In this volume, we are simply trying to gather up the strands of what we have been in the past, in order to realise more fully what we can be in the future. With that idea in mind, there are three reasons for our claim on Geordies.

First, there is no definitive meaning to the name 'Geordie' anyway. As a place to start, Newcastle City Libraries' 'Fact Sheet Number 5', *Origin of the Name Geordie*, offers four original meanings: a supporter of the Hanoverians from the time of the 1745 Jacobite Rising; a name given to coalminers; the nickname for George Stephenson's pit safety lamp; and a term for the Tyneside dialect dating back to Stephenson's oral evidence to Parliamentary enquiries in 1826. A feature in the *Sunday Sun* in March 1964[2] adds two further meanings to the list: the crews of collier vessels, or all those people born within three miles of the banks of the Tyne from Shields to Hexham. *Northern Notes* for 1967[3] adds five more origins: a Greek verb, a Latin adjective, three coins, an unsafe vessel or a two-masted brig. For our purposes here, references to miners or Tynesiders, or some mixture of the two, are the most relevant. Most of them stem from the late nineteenth century, when their meanings were rendered formal in dictionaries and glossaries. Heslop was very clear: '*Geordy*, the name by which Tynesiders are known outside the district'; or a name for pitmen, replacing 'Cranky''in later times' and used by people in South Tynedale for Tyneside pitmen who had moved up the valley for work.[4] Heslop's references were related to actual usage, although it still remains difficult to judge from his work the word's origins or popularity. A glossary of 'Northumbrian Words' was first started by the English Dialect Society, whose members noted down, 'on the spot', words 'customarily heard in the social life of Tyneside, among the hills and dales of Northumberland, and in the fields and working-places of the district'. Then Joseph Cowen heard about the project, and, from 8 October 1887, exposed its researches in the weekly columns of his Newcastle newspaper:

> In this instance the medium proved to be the very best that could have been adopted. Through the pages of the *Chronicle* the list was submitted in detail to the scrutiny of innumerable readers intimately acquainted with and naturally jealous of the correct rendering of their mother tongue.[5]

Heslop wrote up the findings, publishing his *Glossary* in two volumes in 1892.

Usage is one thing, but popular usage is another. From 1905 to 1924, the Newcastle press used every other description but 'Geordie' to report the triumphs of Newcastle United and its supporters:

they were by turns 'Tynesiders', 'Novocastrians', 'Northumbrians', 'Magpies'. 'North-country men', 'Newcastle excursionists'
or 'Northerners', but not Geordies. The same situation obtained for
local regiments at the Somme in 1916 and the Jarrow Marchers
assembling in 1936 – even though J. B. Priestley had used the
name, briefly, in his celebrated *English Journey* two years previously.[6] It seems, then, that 'Geordie' was possibly first used by
outsiders, and that it was associated with pitmen or with Tynesiders assumed to share the characteristics of pitmen (to outside ears,
in the dialect?) on a limited scale, until the name came to be used
more widely in recent times to mean people in general from the
Tyne or the wider region. The BBC Home Service programme
Wotcheor Geordie was immensely popular from 1947, and carried as
its signature tune Jack Robson's 'Wherever ye gan you're sure to
meet a Geordie'. In 1951, a letter to Jack Common made reference
to 'Geordie-land'. When the President of the Northumberland and
Durham Association delivered his inaugural address in London in
1957, he said that being a Geordie went 'beyond mere geography'
and was 'a quality of heart'.[7]

Second, if there is not and never has been a definitive meaning,
there seems to be no good reason why popular usage should not be
recognised. After all, meanings associated with the coalfield always
included Northumberland and Durham, and, more important still,
if we do not claim the meaning now, it might be lost or abused.
'Geordies' could further degenerate into stereotyped joke figures,
usually daft males, or, worse still, they could be turned into boring
topics of after-dinner erudition – 'Did you know that a true "Geordie" was worth a guinea?' 'I think not; a true "Geordie" was a
supporter of the Hanoverians.' Let us seize the moment now to take
the name and dignify ourselves. As the region's pitmen are few in
number, and as the dialect refuses, as usual, to be pinned down to
some linguistic ghetto, and as even in Gosforth there are not many
outspoken Hanoverians left (some would disagree), now seems as
good a time as any to reclaim 'Geordies' for the whole North-East.

There is nothing new in such deeds of repossession. When in
1883 Aaron Watson wrote his chapter on the Tyne for *The Magazine
of Art*, he asked who could imagine that a river with 'the reputation
of being the most depressing stream in Europe' could have had
such a noble history? Well, Watson could, for, as he said, 'Only one
who knows it intimately would confess to an affection for a river like

this'.[8] Watson set about restoring its reputation in his repossession of its history – and in this he was not alone. The regional intelligentsia were doing the same for 'Northumbria' as a whole, and by 1914 they had succeeded in reinventing the region's meaning to itself and to others. This book stands in a tradition.

For regions, no less than nations, are imagined communities. Who the Geordies are depends upon who they imagine themselves to be. The 'North-East' is essentially a state of mind to do with histories and feelings about itself. Newcomers to the region can at first find this state of mind daunting, but in fact Geordie culture is not a culture of exclusivity. Geordie identity has been under pressure for long enough to know that belonging is an act of affiliation and not of birth. Also, of course, Geordies are comers and goers too: the nineteenth century saw very high levels of immigration into the region[9]; and in the twentieth century Geordies have known, more than most, what it is like to be away. For ethnic as opposed to individual settlement, the North-East's track record has been good. The region has absorbed a significant Catholic Irish population, largely without the evils of religious-ethnic sectarianism which have afflicted other places. In Chapter 8, Barry Carr suggests that the South Shields Arabs have come to be seen, and accepted, as Geordies as well as Arabs. Geordie culture is generous and has drawn, and continues to draw, on the generosity of other cultures. As anyone who has been in the region for five minutes will tell you, everyone gets called into the conversation. The question here is to get that conversation to look at its own interests. The North-East's interests, as indicated on a compass-reading from London, are derivative. Given other ways of looking, that could change. And this is the third reason for our claim on Geordies. We want them to turn their face to a new future.

The future from present perspectives looks bleak. The North-East finds itself as the forgotten corner of a British nation-state which, after Raymond Williams, is both too big and too small for the job it has to do: too big to govern effectively (with due representation and understanding), and too small to do what a state needs to do (on a European scale) to ensure the decent and equal welfare of its citizens. Against the centralised nation-state and its absolutist claims, we recommend a federation of *the regions*. We do this because we see the region as a knowable imagined community, small enough to allow democracies to function, and not big enough to let them damage each other. British national identity resides in the south of England.[10] The North-East's human and material resources have been squandered because it is invited to share an identity which imagines that the real nation lives somewhere else. We have to reclaim our resources in order to govern ourselves properly and appropriately. Those who can remember, complain about the loss of 'community spirit'. They talk as if this is inevitable, something to do with 'modern life'. *But it doesn't have to be.* Any system of government which allows such a precious resource to be wasted has lost its claim to govern well. From the emptiness of run-down housing estates, to the total absence of direct British regional representation at Brussels, it is time to recognise that there is a connection between people's feelings for a place and the quality of democratic government which that place enjoys. In fact, in politics, this is the only connection that matters.

We recommend *regions* also as the best units for sustainable economic growth. As with 'community', the North-East has tended to believe that there is a dreadful inevitability about its economic decline. It is as if this is a price that Geordies must pay: that former success created pride, and pride must be punished. Once more, we have to say that this erosion of pride has been a disgraceful squandering of our resources. *Again, it doesn't have to be like this.* In other countries, regional industrial pride has been valued and put to work. In Germany, for instance, the federal system has devolved political power and buoyed-up regional economies. There, it is unconstitutional to permit regional living standards – and therefore markets – to fall below 'national' levels. Moreover, it is understood that market and non-market institutions will work together. Their trade unions are incomparably stronger. Their industrial apprenticeships are integrated into the local economy and earn a level of respect unthinkable here. Their banks are more geared to the needs of manufacturers. Firms, government agencies and educational institutions 'network' one with another to spread innovation, and the German experience is that all this is done best at the regional level. For those who know their history, these are not German ideas as such. Joseph Cowen, the Newcastle MP and industrialist, realised many years ago that markets, governments and civic institutions had to work together to promote economic and social wellbeing. His populist radicalism espoused the North-East as the birthplace of liberty and as the cradle of industrialisation, and he always insisted that the two achievements were not separate. Cowen, 'the Blaydon Brick', recognised that the people of his region were the makers of wealth and the bearers of his hopes. His speeches were in the dialect. He and his working-class allies refused to accept dominant versions of Englishness where working-class people were strangers in their own country while other people ran the place. Current attacks on European federalisation stem from this exclusive view of national identity. Those who run the place, incompetently, as a centralised and secretive nation-state, attack federalism only as a way of defending their own swollen powers. Looking anew and thinking laterally about our place in Europe, Geordies are coming to see that for too long the needs of the South-East have been a brake on their skills and talents. Geordies are waking up to a world wider than the south-bound trip to London to beg for jobs and out-relief. Talk is now of a broad Northern Arc where the Channel Tunnel is left to a congested south, while Geordies break free for trade routes their forebears knew – out of Ireland, and Scotland, and across into Scandinavia, the Baltic, Russia.

'Geordie', you may have noticed, is a man's name. Since its popularisation to mean the people in general, it has hardly been doubted that 'Geordies' means women too, and certainly no-one doubts it here. Yet the fact that we have to say so points to a problem. The editors had little success in finding women writers who felt they could contribute to what we were trying to do. Suffice to say that their reluctance raises another dimension to regional identity which this book has not been able adequately to explore. Elaine Knox covers a lot of ground and we have tried our best to deal with gender matters, but we still look for female contributions to what we see as the inception of a debate.

Finally, on behalf of our contributors, we would like to thank all those who helped in the making of *Geordies*. Of course, this includes the staff of the libraries and record offices where the work was done, as well as the staff of Edinburgh University Press. Thanks are offered also to our students, our audiences, our colleagues, families and friends; and to those who listened, to those who talked back and especially to those who argued that we were pushing too hard too soon. We are grateful to all of them, and trust that they can see it as their book too. For *Geordies* comes out of shared experiences and builds upon cultural achievements hard won. In their generous outlook and in the long pull of emotional loyalty which they have on one another, Geordies stand poised to renew their fortunes in a fast-changing world. Hopeful about the future, but mindful too of what has often been a dispiriting past, we echo an old man's words to Martin Luther King in the midst of the black civil rights struggle in the United States:

> We ain't what we ought to be and we ain't what we want to be and we ain't what we're going to be. But thank God we ain't what we was.[11]

Robert Colls and Bill Lancaster
June 1992

NOTES

1. C. B. Fawcett, *Provinces of England. A Study of some Geographical Aspects of Devolution* (1919; London: Hutchinson, 1960), pp. 85–8.
2. *Sunday Sun*, 22 March 1964.
3. Miss M. Johnson, ed., *Northern Notes*, vol. 2, part 4, July 1967.
4. R. O. Heslop, *Northumberland Words. A Glossary of Words used in The County of Northumberland and on Tyneside* (London, English Dialect Society: Kegan Paul, Trench, Trubner, 1892), vol. II, p. 321, vol. I p. 196.
5. Ibid., vol. I, p. xxvi.
6. See for instance the *Newcastle Daily Journal*, 27 April 1905, 15 April 1907, 18 March 1908, 4 July 1916, 24 December 1918, 26 April 1924; *Newcastle Daily Chronicle*, 10 July 1916; *Newcastle Journal*, 6 October 1936. Priestley referred to Tyne shipyard workers 'cursing in their uncouth accent': *English Journey* (1934; Penguin, 1977) p. 293. Some dialect stories and poems from around the period do not suggest widespread use. While 'Geordie' is used as a typical Tyneside man's name, references to miners are archetypal. Smith says: 'Tynesiders all the world over are bound together by a common speech', and these are 'the ties that knit *Northerners*' (our italics): J. E. Smith, *Tyneside Dialect Poems. On Topical Subjects* (Newcastle: Northumberland Press, 1923), editorial note. See also W. J. Robson, *The adventures of Jackie Robison. Twenty stories in the Tyneside dialect* (Newcastle: R. Robinson, 1904) – Jackie's mate is called 'Geordie Broon': R. O. Heslop, *Geordy's Last. With rhymes and introductory notes*, by 'Harry Haldane' (*Newcastle Daily Journal*, 1879) – 'Geordy' is a miner.

7.   Letter from Joseph Lawson, of Heaton, to Jack Common, *Jack Common Papers* 58, Library of the University of Newcastle upon Tyne; Mr Russell Storey, chairman of Newcastle city magistrates, *Journal and North Mail*, 18 April 1957.

8.   Aaron Watson, 'The Coaly Tyne', *The Magazine of Art*, vol. VI (1883), p. 115. We are grateful to Keith Snell for this reference.

9.   'Our neighbours on one hand were a dear old Irish couple with the real brogue, and on the other a kindly Northumbrian with a hundred per cent burr. Opposite were Cumberland and Lancashire people and, behind, Wales, Cornwall, and Ireland were represented. There were whole masses of Cumbrians, particularly from the town of my birth.

It was a polyglot population, and the Durham dialect, so marked among the children, did not hold unrivalled sway among their elders.' – Boldon Colliery at the turn of the century: Jack Lawson, *A Man's Life* (London: Hodder & Stoughton, 1946) p. 37.

10.   'I am an outsider also. Tyneside is the antithesis of the Crown Heartland, but a million of the Queen's "subjects" live there. We are outside our own national identity': Peter J. Taylor, 'The English and their Englishness', *Scottish Geographical Magazine*, 1991, vol. 107, no 3, p. 159. See also Robert Colls and Philip Dodd, eds, *Englishness. Politics and Culture 1880–1920* (London: Croom Helm, 1986).

11.   Stephen B. Oates, *Let The Trumpets Sound. The Life of Martin Luther King Jnr* (New York: Harper & Row, 1982), p. 253.

CHAPTER ONE

Born-again Geordies

ROBERT COLLS

THE NORTH REBORN?

IN A SPECIAL 1989 supplement, *The North Reborn. Why We're Proud* ('24 pages every Geordie must read'), the *Newcastle Evening Chronicle* studded every page with headlines no Geordie could miss: 'A Time For Optimism', 'How We Worked Wonders', 'More Jobs', 'Better and Better', 'And We'll Drink To That!' On the front page was a large photograph of Mrs Thatcher.

Nine years earlier, the Director of Leisure and Recreation for Hartlepool had had a different tale to tell:

> But the problem came, what do you really sell about Hartlepool? You know I mean Paris has its Eiffel Tower, Blackpool has its tower, Salisbury has got a cathedral, so what do I say about Hartlepool? . . .

> I think that Hartlepool's councillors were not interested until we put the idea that tourism is an industry. As soon as it dawned on them that it could be promoted as an industrial development, in part, there doesn't seem to be a problem any more; they licked the word 'industry', and so now I always talk of the 'tourist industry', and they quite accept it . . .

> We've lost the chance of the microchip, we lost the titanium plant . . . the steel industry is gone, the only stuff coming in the harbour is service industry, driving motor cars off . . . I accept it's cosmetic . . .

> You know a job is a job. If you need jobs as badly as Hartlepool needs them, I don't really think it matters whether you are throwing molten steel about or you are throwing cups of tea over customers.
> (Northumbria Tourist Board, *Planning for Tourism*, 1980)

It was hard to believe that this account of Hartlepool inhabited the same time and space as the *Chronicle's* North, but the newspaper's editor had the answer. Just beneath the prime minister's right elbow, he opined that

> The difference from twenty years ago is that the region is getting off its backside and doing something about it. The 'Dead, Dark Days', as older inhabitants call them, have been weathered. We have even got through a period when Newcastle United were not in the First Division.

This was less than accurate. Twenty years before, the North-East's economy had been distinctively stronger than it was in 1989 and, soon after the editor's prognosis – as if to typify the region's general economic experience – Newcastle United were back in the Second Division, with their finest ex-players gracing the stadia of other clubs. The *Chronicle's* story did not bear much investigation. Like the government's 1988 white paper on Trade and Industry, it was long on rhetoric and short on policy, regional policy in particular. As the *Northern Economic Review* reported in 1989, the claimed revival of North-East business activity was mainly myth: around forty per cent of the growth in labour demand was due to government work schemes; around forty per cent of the fall in unemployment was due to more severe restrictions on benefit claims; and most of the new jobs were part-time, low-skilled, low-paid, non-union, and in the service sector. Hardly enough to make you proud.

And yet, if the editor's optimism was misconceived, the Leisure Director's pessimism was not quite appropriate either. The North-East *can* have a future which is not its past. In its strong regional coherence and industrial tradition, with local government keen and expert in economic strategy, and in its adaptability to all kinds of manufacturing on a seaboard close to some of the world's most prosperous markets, the North-East has the potential to restore its position as one of the great regional economies of Europe.

So, what can it really mean for the region to be born again? There are two ideas to keep in mind. First, the world is never just as it appears; behind appearances lies an ache to be other than it is, and this ache needs expression. Second, the power to be represented culturally is as important as the power to be represented politically.

However, before we can ask what it means for Geordies to be born again in the 1990s, we have to go back to basics. When did the region first find its modern identity? Why did its inhabitants come to be seen as a distinct people? How much say did they have in the process? By doing so, we will realise that the idea of birth and death has been central from the start – that there has never been a time, in this century at least, when the North-East has not been represented as coming up, going down, or poised uneasily somewhere between the two. Born-again Geordies are nothing new.

BIRTHS AND DEATHS

It was from the 1860s that the North-East found its modern identity. Before then, the eighteenth century is unknown territory, sparsely populated and less able to communicate, while in the early nineteenth century the North-East was dominated by metropolitan perceptions of a 'Great Northern Coalfield' which kept London warm. The later nineteenth century saw the birth of a distinctive regional identity, and this identity was accompanied by momentous developments in industry, communications, population growth and urban living. Prompted by national re-evaluations of what it was to be 'English', the regional intelligentsia struggled to establish their 'northernness'. 'Northernness' was not the same as Englishness. Instead, Northernness was construed, like 'Britishness', as *a peripheral place*, complementary to but not the same as the essentially English heartlands to the south. People started talking again about 'Northumbria'.

'Regionalism' entered the language in 1881. By walking the land and looking at it, and by writing and reading about it, the New Northumbrians rediscovered their region. However we see these activities, the Land and its People became matters of profound concern. What mattered was not in some other place. It became important for New Northumbrians to identify with their region. How they did so, in their minds, is reconstructed here:

The time is any time between 1890 and 1920. Kitted out for hiking, we wait before Alnwick Castle. We are pilgrims of place. Historic Northumbria – ancient kingdom and wellspring of our true selves – is walked by Edmund Bogg in his 1898 Two Thousand Miles of Wandering:

Alnwick

'I never heard the old song of Percy and Douglas, that I found not my heart moved more than with a trumpet.'

Standing before the princely home of the Percies, with the effigies of silent sentinels looking down from the battlements as if watching for the foe, and every other external object bespeaking the greatness and martial fame of the members of the heroic race, I found myself unconsciously repeating the above inspiring and soul-stirring words of that gallant soldier, himself a model of chivalry, Sir Philip Sidney . . .

To us pilgrims, it does not concern us that Alnwick Castle was not the home of the medieval Percies. Nor does it matter that Harry Hotspur could not have known its eighteenth-century battlements. It does not even matter that not all of us are Northumbrians by birth – for we have read our Border Ballads and the Proceedings of Newcastle Lit. and Phil., and all good patriots are welcome to join in our walk. In spite of our historical interests, our real destination is with the present. As we travel the land, so we traverse our minds. In each sacred place where a reverie is induced, the past is fused with the present to form a unity, a unity which the better-read among us recognise as the 'personality' of place. Recognising that personality, and protecting it, is a complex internal process. Trespassers are not welcome. We don't stray too close to urban or industrial areas down among the miners, or along the Tyne or Wear. As amateur students of archaeology, antiquarianism, natural history, local history and the new geography, we find not the region in our studies but our studies in the region, which is the precious focus of all we know. For we come here not as surveyors but as patriots. We are not interested in detail, in measuring tonnage or in inspecting agriculture. Rather, we are here to swoon before an aesthetic which we ourselves have invented. In such a way, squinting in the right light, from the right distance, in the right frame of mind, even 'Industry' can be reclaimed. If part of Northumbria's true personality is warlike, then down on the Tyne, as 'we peer into fitful patches of lurid light', we will find builders of battleships who, hammer in hand, clench the old martial spirit:

The confusion which the noise and bustle of the surrounding scene produce on the mind of the visitor is bewildering, as, from amid the clouds of hissing stream and volcanoes of smoke and flame, comes the roaring of the forge, clanking of steel, rattling of chains, and the reverberations of a thousand hammers wielded by hands engaged in shipbuilding, the howling and panting of blasts and the din of rolling machinery, commingling with the ringing of bells and hoarse shriek of the whistles of passing steamers.

— 4 —

For those of our number who dabble in Eugenics and who worry about the deleterious effects of 'Industry' on the race, workers such as these 'sons of Odin' suggest a strength to survive. The geographers among us know that although the industrial parts are not pretty they are proof of the survival of an old region, now teeming with life and naturalising its own conditions to suit its own energies. As the geographer Vidal de la Blache remarked, such victories are 'won under rare and unusual circumstances', bearing out 'the dominant idea in all geographical progress', 'that of terrestrial unity'.

In carefully constructed textual and actual encounters such as these, the North-East was reborn as a 'terrestrial unity'. Land became homeland, homelands required capitals and, in the week-end ramblings of a new generation of hikers, field watchers, bicy-clists and amateur historians, the City-in-its-Region was discovered. Tomlinson, in his 1889 *Comprehensive Guide*, was moved to poetry by the sight of a regional capital, Newcastle, where, 'Under certain conditions there is a sombre grandeur about these fire-wasted landscapes that appeals with irresistible power to a truly poetic nature'. By 1919, the geographer Fawcett had turned this middle-class imagining into an academic theory. All places were equal, but some places were more *natural* than others. Faw-cett's 'North Country' was both a natural region and conscious of it:

> It is very difficult to make any estimate of the extent and strength of local patriotism in any part of the country. But it does seem to be generally agreed that it is very much stronger in those counties which approximate to natural regions than it is elsewhere. Thus Yorkshire, Lancashire, and Devonshire are counties in which it is strong; while in Surrey, Hertfordshire, and Rutlandshire it appears to be far less important. In some cases the feeling may be associated with a wider region than the county. County patriotism is not prominent in Durham ... Their local patriotism is for the North Country rather than for the county.

Fawcett had been born in Staindrop, County Durham. He divided England into its natural regions based upon six principles of divi-sion, five of which were to do with population settlement and geography, and one to do with 'local patriotism and ... tradition'. He called this exercise 'applied geography' and was very mindful of the political implications of his work. Warning that in the existing boundaries there was 'nothing sacrosanct', he made Newcastle the capital and came up with a 'North Country' comprising North-umberland, Durham, most of Cumberland, North Westmorland and a slice of the North Riding. He thought that this rare mix of natural division and regional patriotism supported a Northern claim to 'provincial self-government'.

So soon after the New Northumbrian life came the death. Reborn as a place of power and personality by 1919, the North-East died during the 1930s. Ellen Wilkinson's Jarrow was the town that was 'murdered'; the Pilgrim Trust's Crook was inert; J. B. Priestley's Gateshead was derelict, Shotton he had to exhume from the waste and sulphur of its own labour, and the Tyne was a pool of rust. The decisions that mattered had been taken in some other place. It became important to reidentify with a region which had been laid low. The New Northumbrians were replaced by a new generation of regionalists:

The time is any time between 1930 and 1939. Dressed for reporting – notebook, camera, questionnaire, addresses, useful numbers – we move through A Special Area. We are pilgrims of the national conscience. Dining out by Tyne and Wear, humbled by what was once proud, we view our own rivers of guilt. J. B. Priestley, in his English Journey, *is one of us:*

> Grim and ugly as it might be, nevertheless if this riverside had been black and shattering with the smoke and din of tens of thousands of men hard at it, for the commonwealth and for their own decent comfort and self-respect, I think I would have found it wildly inspiring, a scene to overtop any poor praise of mine. There was, of course, some good work going on, but what chiefly caught the eye there were evidences of past greed, now satiated here and ravening elsewhere, and present indifference and neglect.

To us pilgrims, it does not matter that there had never been a time when tens of thousands of men had been 'hard at it' for a 'commonwealth'. Nor does it matter that few of us are Geordies, for we have heard of a Depression in the North and all good patriots must be told the horror. In spite of our current concern with unemployment, our thoughts are in the past. As we move among the victims, so we examine our past lives. Some of that examination is to do with nationhood, some with class inequality, and some to do with ourselves as men. In each broken place where self-examination is induced, the present is fused with the past to form a unity, a unity which the left-wingers among us recognise as the Historic Failure of Capitalism. Recognising that Failure, and apportioning blame, is a complex internal process. Self-blame is diminished by being here, and being concerned; the blame of others is implied by their not being here and not being concerned. Although middle class ourselves, we don't stray too close to middle-class, ex-urban or suburban gentilities in Hexham or Gosforth. As the Fortunate People – taller, healthier, better-dressed, with proper voices from other places – we document the opposite of our own good fortune in the grim reality of this region. As watchers of the Less Fortunate People, we look down on them in order to concoct our remedies – communism, socialism, realism, charity, decency, dignity, emigration; in particular, 'work'. We are here to trudge before the shame we feel. Done in the right way, with the right tone, in the right light, and seen from without, even middle- or upper-class guilt can be assuaged. If the North-East's present is emasculated, then its past was strong and all the stronger for being able to do without the likes of us. Priestley admits it:

> I could not lend a hand with that work, but let nobody assume for a moment that I cannot appreciate its grim strength and mastery, its Promethean and Vulcanic grandeur, or that I moved through this setting for it like a flinching minor poet dreaming of roses. Labour of this kind, bending iron and riveting steel to steel, is the real thing, man's work.

For those of our number who dabble in revolutionary politics, 'these Geordies, stocky toothless fellows in caps and mufflers', suggest a manhood born to fight. With John Grierson, the documentary film-maker, the socialists are sure that the 'great days of unmitigated individualism and governmental laissez-faire are over . . . the day of common unified planning has arrived'.

Reborn by 1919, dead by 1934, the region was reborn again after 1945 – spectacularly so in local Labour politician T. Dan Smith's planning hopes for a Newcastle as 'the Brasilia of the North'. Then, in the early 1980s, the North-East died again, this time on a scale of manufacturing decline commensurate with, or even worse than, the 1930s. Between 1978 and 1984, thirty-eight per cent of Tyne-side's manufacturing employment was wiped out. For the region as a whole, the *Employment Gazette* for November 1989 reported that, since 1978, jobs in manufacturing had fallen from 415,000 to 282,000, while jobs in the primary sector had fallen from 93,000 to 49,000. The traditional industries – coalmining, shipbuilding and repair, marine engineering, heavy engineering – went into serious, and in some places terminal, decline. The communities and skills that went with them were dislocated too. What manufacturing capacity remained was mainly branch plant assembly. By the mid-1980s, the service sector accounted for nearly seventy per cent of all employment in the region, and the rates of unemployment were the highest in Britain. In 1986, the trade unions tried to re-enact the Jarrow March. One death was used to stir the embers of another.

So many deaths. So many rebirths. But which was which? It is at times hard to tell. Old endings have so often been taken to signify new beginnings, old memories to transform new experiences, that the sense of time becomes skewed. In addition, as in the rhetoric of all 'little nations', it is said that the *essential* region – same land, same people – goes on just the same.

PLANNERS

Whatever the truth of people's real lives and opportunities, it was clear that, after the war, those with the power to pronounce on such things deemed that another new beginning had to be made. If Fawcett's 1919 proposal for regional government was the first watershed, William Geenty's 1951 Durham *County Development Plan* was the second. The *Plan* was in no doubt that a break with the past was necessary. Against the 'slow harmonious growth' of previous centuries, the *Plan* argued that industrialisation had come to 'ignore the contours', cause 'disfigurements' and deposit 'an ugly imposition' like 'a rash' with 'irreparable gashes', on a land 'polluted' and 'fouled'. With the public sector in apparent economic and political control, there was little need for image-building here. The harsh truth could be told, and the truth was that the region had to be replanned in order to be reborn. After the war, two generations of architects went into the public sector as Utopian visionaries. The old environment was to be swept away; a new world was to be built. But George Oldham, Newcastle City Architect, recalled this dream of starting from scratch as a tale of misspent youth. In 1986 at the Newcastle 'Environment 2000 Seminar', he spoke for many in his profession when he admitted that a new land for a new people had not worked according to plan; his 'Brave New World' had not been achieved. What had gone wrong?

What had gone wrong was that the people of the region had only rarely been invited to their own wakes and christenings. Since the

1860s, they had won political representation but not much in the
way of cultural representation. Consider the first Northumbrian
rebirth. Amid all that celebration of race force and martial spirit,
there was no talk of death and disease. Whatever the New Northumbrians imagined they saw, their sons of Odin were dying of
bronchitis and TB in the most overcrowded homes in England. The
image did not fit the reality. Or consider the first Geordie death.
Many of those who represented the regional culture in the 1930s
did so by assuming that dreariness of landscape meant the dreariness of the people who lived in it. So closely had the landscape been
connected with the people, and both with a regional 'personality',
that the spoliation of one was seen as the actual ruination of all. Bill
Brandt's camera, a dissonant lens schooled in the Parisian surreal-
ist studios of the 1920s, came north to show the nation the region. It
duly showed places and people, a dark side of the landscape, in
depression.

To be sure, the interwar years brought many more social
problems and intensified existing ones. As the depression
deepened, H. A. Mess's *Industrial Tyneside*, published in 1928,
laid the basis for further investigations into health, housing and
poverty. In 1934 and 1939, Newcastle Corporation investigated
the health and nutrition of infants. In 1940, David Goodfellow's
research group (*Tyneside. The Social Facts*) built upon Mess's earlier
work to reveal a region seriously disadvantaged in almost every
aspect of social well-being. Unemployment, tuberculosis, infant
mortality, malnutrition and overcrowding were all well above the
national average. In 1938, for the poorest London borough, Shore-
ditch, 137 out of every 10,000 inhabitants were on unemployment
assistance; in Hebburn, the figure was 485. Between 1935 and
1937, Tyneside suffered seventy-two per cent more deaths from TB
than London, and fifty-nine per cent more than the national average. The list was long and the impoverishment shocking. Industrial
collapse, bad housing, a blighted landscape – this was hard tack for
the national conscience. Place and people remained as 'one', but,
whereas the New Northumbrians had put them in the light of
regional power, the interwar investigators put them in the shadow
of regional depression. Once, the North-East had been seen as a
place of energy and self-making. Now it was seen as sick and in need
of help.

In providing that help, even the working-class's own history came to be ranged against them. Durham's *Development Plan* wanted to move 290,743 people. In order to do so, it had to devalue the worth of those places where many of them lived. The Hammonds' famous working-class history, *The Town Labourer* (1917), was used by the *Plan* not for that sense of relationship and self-making which was its hallmark, but simply for 'conditions' – 'long, monotonous rows', 'bare minimum of accommodation', 'whole environment ... mechanical and dreary'. The little working-class self-making that was invoked in the *Plan* was taken from the miners' histories of Richard Fynes and Sidney Webb, but once again in the 1951 version the struggle had been totally lost; the miners had been pushed down into an abyss of low pay, contractual serfdom, isolated villages, no culture, little recreation, bad health, ignorance: 'At work, home, or play, the miner could not escape the absolute domination of the mine owner'. Richest insult of all, Keir Hardie's words were taken out of context and used to silence the *Plan*'s critics. Had not the miners' own champion warned against 'The weight of the dead past in the miner's mind ...?' So much for the past. For the present, the *Plan* relied largely upon Priestley, an outsider who had come and gone some fifteen years before, in the teeth of the depression.

Regeneration was not simply a political problem. Durham County Council was Labour-controlled and, more than that, it was dominated by the National Union of Mineworkers. The problem was cultural too, in that the planners' ambitions involved ways of seeing the people that did not necessarily accord with the people's ways of seeing themselves. In the new region – a neat and orderly landscape dotted with public welfare agencies and social amenities – those who did not fit would have to change, or move. In this sense it was, and is, too easy to blame a 'them' in the south, with political power and capital, who manipulated an 'us' in the north. When in 1947 the Town and Country Planning Act required councils to formulate a development plan, that 'them' in the south was a Labour government with decent intentions and regional policies. They thought they could use the state to override the whims of private capital and cushion the impact of the market. On these assumptions, they believed that long-term trends could be planned. So had the interwar investigators believed. So did the Durham *Plan*. 'Coal is fundamental ...' it said, and, with the NUM at its right hand and the NCB at its left, it clearly believed that

politics could displace economics. A totally controlled people, once
domineered over by tyrants and the business cycle, the men and
women of County Durham would now be organised by good fellows
and sound planning. Even where the achievements of the people in
their own representation were recognised ('tremendous class-consciousness, comradeship and solidarity'), in a planned future such
achievements had to be explained away. They did not fit the trends.

So, 1951 was a time to be born again. Conditions would replace
relationships, planning would replace chaos, and consumption
would replace production. That rich associational life which the
communities had produced would have to be given up and, in the
name of a new beginning, the *County Development Plan* pronounced
sentence of death on some 117 settlements and the deliberate
run-down of twenty-nine others. Although, as Geenty warned, the
new towns would raise 'a major problem of reintegration and
rehabilitation' – what their first generation of residents called 'New
Town Blues' – his *Plan* paid little more than lip service to what
the old settlements had already achieved in terms of community-
building. So much was missed. So much was squandered. It was as
if 'comradeship and solidarity' were independent variables. The
death villages were assigned 'Category D' status.

With the run-down of coalmining in the 1950s, and again under a
Labour government in the 1960s, a whole generation of North-East
writers and artists would dwell on what had been lost. While they
worried about whether such things could be made again, there
were others who were keen to represent the death as a rebirth. T.
Dan Smith thought that 'The sooner all the mines were closed the
better it would be', and Graham Turner found the people of Witton
Park lacking in the true spirit of their region:

> They were clinging to the past, to something that was dying, to a
> tight, cosy, clammy little world where there was nothing new or
> adventurous or bracing, nothing of the challenge which had made
> their grandfathers such resilient men ... '– there's an awful lot of
> Celtic twilight around the place.'

PATRONS

Ashington in Northumberland might have been described as such
a 'clammy little world'. In 1937, the Shell Guide listed it as a

'Mining town (pop. 40,000) mostly built in the early part of this century. Dreary rows a mile long. Ashpits and mines down the middle of still unmade streets.' Places like this might produce workers and footballers, but painters never, still less a group of painters now recognised by their historian William Feaver as a significant part of twentieth-century British painting, still less a group of painters who, from their first WEA meeting in October 1934 to the demolition of their hut in October 1983, went their own way.

Given the prevailing claims on the regional culture and its representation, what could the Ashington painters do but retain their independence? Miners were there to be painted, perhaps, but they were not supposed to do the painting. As Jan Gordon said in 1934 of how to paint 'Miners Coming Back from Work in the Dusk', do them 'with simple lines, merged masses, dim colours ...'. This was not original advice. A hundred years of painting had done it this way. From Henry Perlee Parker in the 1830s; to the Royal Commission artists, the *Illustrated London News*, and T. H. Hair in the 1840s; to the *Graphic* thereafter and many of those genre painters, illustrators, photographers, realists, war artists and documentarists who followed, miners were given their place in a moral *chiaroscuro* of light and shade. Parker's 1836 'Pitmen Playing Quoits' depicted them as blackened, Moorish brigands (see Figure 1.1); Clausen's 1924 London Midland Scottish poster, 'Coal', depicted them as cloth-capped apes. Thomas Hair was the first artist to concentrate on the North-East's pits but, as his associate admitted, 'Few persons, even of those resident in the coal district, are possessed of sufficient nerve to descend a pit' – yet, once down, they would find 'a scene as wild and fearful as a painter or a poet could wish to see'. And what the painter wished to see was something not normally encountered. When the Duchess of Northumberland went on her picturesque tour of the county in 1760, she asked her diary how she would choose to experience her encounters with the abnormal. Would she choose to feel them as 'cheerful melancholy romantic wild or dreary?' A century later, painters of industrial encounters would do the same. 'Labour' and 'Industry' emerged as categories of emotional and aesthetic response. Thus, William Bell Scott would be drawn to that Tyneside 'Labour' so different from his own which he chose as 'characteristic of the district', Frank Brangwyn would be praised as the nation's translator of 'the

FIGURE I.I: '... blackened, Moorish brigands.' *Pitmen Playing Quoits* (1840), Oil painting, Henry Perlee Parker (1795–1873); Laing Art Gallery, Newcastle upon Tyne (Tyne and Wear Museums).

Dignity of Labour' and Sir Charles Holmes as 'the inventor of the Industrial Landscape', while official War Artist John Lavery would find in Elswick munitions factories subjects so 'very different from his usual fashionable clientele'. As the Harrieses tell us in their *The War Artists* (1983), Kenneth Clark said his artists journeyed to the front to find there 'some of that emotional stimulus on a grand scale which is inevitably lacking from [their] everyday work'. Mines, factories and shipyards were part of that 'front' too, and along with regions of a similar cast, the North-East became the *other* place, the place where painters would find something different.

Given the strangeness of the encounter, the rates of exchange between the region and its representors were never equal. A place for the jaded emotions or social guilt of outsiders, they came to stand on the edge, feeling strange, looking for themselves. During the war, Graham Sutherland encountered in a Cornish tin mine 'a world of such beauty and such mystery', Henry Moore rediscovered in a Yorkshire coal mine his 'humanist side', and Stanley Spencer encountered in a Glasgow shipyard a new home 'dark and cosy', 'a certain atmosphere which I feel a need for in myself'. Just before the war, in December 1938, the North-East attracted similar attention when the Mass Observation collaborator Humphrey Spender went to Newcastle for the *Daily Mirror* and *Picture Post*. For the *Mirror*, he was expected to take pleasant photographs. For the *Post*, Spender was able to give vent to his bourgeois guilt with a 'realism so harsh that we evoked a strong complaint from the mayor'. Meanwhile, another Mass Observer, the young Northumbrian aristocrat Julian Trevelyan, also found in the North-East that which he needed to find. Jeremy Mulford records in his *Worktown People* (1982) that, having flirted with communism, called himself a socialist, joined the Artists International and badgered his friends in high places about the fascist threat, Trevelyan came to the point where

> All this now seemed quite useless, and it was more by way of the enthusiasm of the Ashington miners for their paintings that I regained my faith in the more permanent values of our civilisation . . .

Even from their friends, the Ashington painters had to beware of strangers bearing gifts. Tom Harrison brought a crate of beer. Harrison, the founder of Mass Observation and the anthropologist of proletarian 'tribal life', was keen to do the right thing in a strange land. Hotfoot from a BBC talk on 'Art and the Working Chap', Harrison came to Ashington to meet the Great Proletarian Painter. Most of the group didn't drink. Robert Lyon brought not beer but his training. Lyon, the group's founder and university tutor, a man who knew their work better than any other outsider, could never quite see that work as other than 'naïve', as an exercise under uncultured conditions. Others brought gallery space. The Director of the National Gallery in Edinburgh put their work on a par with a recent exhibition by Boys' Clubs. Again, simple expression under unlikely conditions. The anti-fascist British Artists' Congress put them on the third floor of its Grosvenor Square mansion, in their place with 'Working Men's Groups'. 'Surrealism' got the ballroom. As manual workers, the Ashington Miners' art could not be reflective: it had to be primitive, without thought. As painters who stayed, in the region, in their homes, in their jobs, their art could not address the universal: it had to be provincial.

The North-East has been seen, therefore, not only as an abnormal place to which one travelled in order to be bitten by the surroundings, but also as a working-class region whose ability to know and represent itself outside itself was questionable. Audiences in the North-East never dreamed of seeing themselves at the movies but, when they did, they didn't (see Figure 1.2). A. J. Cronin's *The Stars Look Down* (1939) was not filmed in the region, and Michael Redgrave and Emlyn Williams were given the parts of Northumberland pitmen. American critics thought the film was

FIGURE 1.2: 'Audiences in the North-East never dreamed of seeing themselves at the movies, but when they did, they didn't.' *Zion Hall, South Shields* (1933), Photograph: South Tyneside Libraries.

about South Wales. Welsh film historians still think it was about County Durham.

Taken together, the abnormality of the region and its inability to know itself were forms of disenfranchisement. As with the planners, the patrons would speak for you. At best, the Ashington painters were thought able to express only what was familiar, and, because that was considered limited, so must be its representation. At worst, because everyone knew that Art was separate from Industry, that it was something which had to be brought in from the outside, the Ashington men were an anomaly in need of explanation. Leading critics like Roger Fry (*Vision and Design* 1929) saw true artists as a species of free-floating aesthetes enjoying 'a life freed from the binding necessities of our actual existence'. According to Fry, the true artist was distinct 'in his whole attitude to life', his emotions were apart – 'as remote from actual life and its practical utilities as the most useless mathematical theory'. Such an artist could connect with everyday existence only briefly, and only then for the purposes of 'Art'. This was not how the Ashington painters saw their work. They stood their ground, stayed waged labourers, formed their artists' lodge, painted when they could, took what learning was acceptable, and refused what they saw as the Arts Council's invitations to be exemplary northerners, refused to be impressed by Henry Moore's lumpy figures, refused to represent the region as in its death throes and refused to be separated from their subjects. In both Planning and Art, there were, and are, similar assumptions at work. Planners and patrons consistently undervalued what they heard and what they saw. Local knowledge was confined to simple things expressed in simple ways. The parts could never be considered capable of that wholeness which the patrons claimed to possess. Close rather than detached, reflexive rather than informed, local knowledge was in some way incomplete. By stubbornly holding on to their independence, the Ashington painters were bidding for wholeness. In doing so, like the people of the North-East at the hands of the planners, they were distanced from their real achievements by a complex and beguiling system of cultural patronage.

In literature also there was patronage. Oliver Kilbourn and the Ashington group stayed where they were; Jack Common, on the other hand, moved out. Leaving Newcastle to ply his trade among London left-wing literary circles in the 1930s, Common won minor recognition as a talented writer whose major achievement was yet to come. Throughout this time, he drew the most beguiling cultural patronage that a self-educated, working-class Tynesider could expect. To George Orwell, he was a friend as well as a writer 'of proletarian origin' and a 'proletarian viewpoint' who wrote in the spirit of 'the quieter corners of the four ale bar on a Saturday night'. To E. M. Forster, he was 'a warm-hearted, matey writer' of the sort who might do socialism some good. To the anonymous reviewer 'H. F.', 'Common' could not be a proper name in a leftie book; the real author might be the socialist intellectual and Oxford don, Dick Crossman. For the sculptor Lawrence Bradshaw, Common's brow structure served as the model for Karl Marx's in Highgate Cemetery – the sculptor said he found there a similar patience and understanding.

When in 1951 Jack Common's major achievement finally came with the publication of *Kiddar's Luck*, the book was misunderstood. Like the Ashington paintings, the book was seen as unusual: unusual because it was the product of a working-class author, unusual because it dealt with out-of-the-way experiences, unusual because it appeared to achieve 'art' without artifice. As such, *Kiddar's Luck* was bracketed in the vaguely northern, curiously simple, lyrically poor-but-happy genre. Within this code, 'northern' meant regional, regional meant working-class and, for the working-class author or painter – almost a contradiction in terms in some circles – this meant someone who inevitably looked back, back at what he had been but no longer was. Common's past, his tribe in its 'Dead End' of 'back-street realism', was 'real life', 'just banged down', 'slice by slice . . . a very simple story, hardly a story at all, of home life'. In these respects, Common's Newcastle was not unlike the painters' Ashington – a place passed by, unusual, warm and naive. Such reviews were by no means intended as criticisms, but they missed the measure of Common's achievement. Especially, they missed its life and its universality. Common's book did not depict the regionality of the region as a static thing, either in topography or custom or days gone by; instead he depicted region- ality through moving and living gestures, its mentality and its idiom. Nor did Common's book content itself with regional matters alone. Instead he offered an anlysis of capitalism as a life-denying system based on time discipline – a sort of death wish which finds its way into the most sensitive areas of human relationship, the more so for those who exact the discipline.

After years of waiting for something else, for The Great Proletarian Novel, the left-wing intelligentsia did not recognise *Kiddar* when it came. It was good of its type, but its type was limited. The *Daily Worker* was especially unforgiving. Common was remembered as someone who had been paraded around literary parties as the 'Working Man Author', a rebuke which, no matter how apposite for the party-givers, was bitter comment indeed for an author who in 1951 lived in a council house and who earned a living digging by day and writing by night. The *Daily Worker* did not think that the book was intended for the workers: the book lacked political theory and was cynical. Had not its author said that 'a good political conscience' was 'an excellent foundation for adultery'? Of course, this newspaper was not noted for its irony, and Common was the master of it. Perhaps his communist reviewer remembered the games he had played with bourgeois left and right alike?

CURE FOR BOURGEOISERIE

How? If you have any reason to suspect yourself of being bourgeois in some way, if your bowels are sluggish, if you have a tendency to sell things or to save money, if you find yourself attached to your possessions or interested in credit schemes, if you think you would like to lead the workers, then you cannot do better than take a good stiff dose of anti-bourgeois cathartic. This is the invention of Karl Marx, a man himself considerably afflicted ...

(*New Britain*, 11 April, 1934)

Kiddar's Luck found praise, but not for what it was. He received his patrons' due yet, in the end, the book was stuffed away. Proletarian novels, like proletarian paintings, were either not artistic or not artistic enough. Regional novels, like regional paintings, were either of their place and in their place knowing only that, or they were parochial. The wayward *Kiddar* confounded these conventions. It was not until 1968 that someone said what had really been achieved. Sid Chaplin understood the author, his people, their bittersweet way with irony and the forms of patronage which had misplaced and lost their masterpiece. As for Common himself, he ended his days where his hero Will Kiddar had begun, down on his luck. Willing Employer Wanted.

A MALE RESPONSE

Whatever the ways in which the planners and patrons sought to represent the region on the region's behalf, there can be no doubt that the abiding issues were men's issues. When the patrons wanted to place the region's culture, they did so as men thinking of what was appropriate to masculine identities. When the planners wanted to regenerate the region's life in the 1950s, they did so as men thinking of masculine degeneration in the 1930s. A region of male workers who realised themselves through their labour, the region's personality was bound up with their manhood. Since the 1930s, the dominant way of representing North-East birth and death has hung on the heroic image of the male worker in or out of a job. Given the power of this image to stand for the region as a whole, and its resilience up to our own time, we have to ask how much life is left in it. How strong does the male response remain?

Sid Chaplin once referred to a collection of photographs of the lodge banners of the Durham coalfield as '*the* family album'. Again, Chaplin got it right. He understood the banner as people's art and he knew that it sprang out of trade unionism in one moment of history, as a genuinely popular movement. Marching in their communities, behind their lodge banner, the people of the coalfield carried an iconography of 'Labour' and 'Industry' which projected a larger association of some dignity. For a time, around the turn of the century, an art expressing such a dignity came to stand for the region. Unquestionably the most popular North-East painter during this period, Ralph Hedley first exhibited at the Royal Academy in 1879. Hedley's patrons were middle class. They liked his broad, familiar landscapes, his painting of useful, decent folk. But there is evidence that the working class liked his work too. His art was equally at home above the cottage mantelpiece. The *Newcastle Weekly Chronicle*, newspaper of the coalfield, did a brisk trade in Hedley chromolithographs. Hedley's life spanned the years of industrial transformation. Two years before he died, in 1911, nearly half of County Durham's labour force were employed in only four great male sectors – iron, shipbuilding, coal and engineering. His people were men brought out of the darkness into the light. The light was one of self-recognition: their associational life was never far away; their basic worth was ever present. If the radical Newcastle MP and owner of the *Chronicle*, Joseph Cowen,

FIGURE 1.3: '... selling Cowen's papers, no doubt, was an exploited child in wet sackcloth.' *The Newsboy* (1892), Watercolour, Ralph Hedley (1848–1913): Laing Art Gallery, Newcastle upon Tyne (Tyne and Wear Museums).

had ever required a court painter, Hedley would have been his man. But not cravenly so. *The Newsboy* (1892), selling Cowen's papers no doubt, was an exploited child in wet sackcloth (see Figure 1.3). Hedley's work was cultural franchise of a sort, yet, as in politics, it was exercised not by but on behalf of the working class and restricted itself to male accomplishments. In his *Geordie Ha'ad the Bairn* (1890), a painting inspired by a Joe Wilson song 'Aw Wish yor Muther wad Cum', even child care became the pitman's prerogative. A rare picture of a man with child, Hedley's depiction turned a music-hall joke into a scene of proletarian male tenderness, a male Madonna. Never a New Northumbrian (he preferred contemporary themes), nor an aesthete (he was a wood-carver and saw no reason to leave his business or his region), Hedley was nevertheless capable of sentiment about a class he admired. Like the best 'realist' genre painters of his day, Herkomer, Brangwyn or those *Graphic* artists who so influenced Van Gogh, Ralph Hedley did not paint the labour movement as such, but he did paint with a strong sense of working-class achievement around him.

What sort of achievement was this? One central feature was Labour's claim on the region as its own estate. The firms which caught the imagination – Swan Hunter's, or Palmer's, or Armstrong's, or the great colliery and railway combines – were big and labour-intensive, with dense concentrations of skilled men. One did not have to be a political economist to see that these men mattered. And in labour organisation, no other region compared. Two of the greatest trade unions, the miners and boilermakers, were strong, and in other organisations too – the Labour Party, the Cooperative movement, the Friendly Societies, the Clubs and Institutes – Labour was trying to secure its interests. Its prime interest, of course, was The Trade. Trade interests were regional interests, or, to put it another way, during the second half of the nineteenth century a number of skilled, well-organised and interconnected male occupations came to be seen as the direct expression of the North-East itself. The major Trades worked the region's natural resources, and their 'tradesmen' saw themselves as the men who turned those resources into wealth. In shipbuilding, the craft unions operated by River. This 'River' was first and foremost a river of work, of custom and practice hard won and translated into the rulebook. When trade was bad, when the 'River' was 'flat' – and that was often in a fluctuating market – then the whole locality suffered. In the Coal and Shipbuilding Trades, the various arbitration and conciliation boards all sought to emphasise the interdependence of capital and labour, although in terms of their joint responsibility to the region the unions were in no doubt as to who was the steadier partner. Capital was wayward; it could be tyrannical or irresponsible, and socialists denied its role altogether; but, this side of the revolution, a sort of partner it had to remain. Labour on the other hand saw itself as representing the region's best interests: Labour was rooted, Labour was the majority, Labour was democratic. As the voice of the people, its task was to civilise and defend their home.

Closely connected with the interests of The Trade was the political rhetoric of The People. This was the *true* People, a historic formation invoked by most radical liberal, labour and socialist parties and programmes. Having suffered grievously at Tyranny's hand, The People were now building their path to salvation. The path was broad and open for those manly enough to take it. Nowhere more so, or so the rhetoric went, than in the 'North'. Here, everywhere one looked there was resurgence, a resurgence often contrasted with the privilege and parasitism of an effete and spurious 'South'. Most importantly, The People were industrious and enterprising and had the tonnage and moral culture to prove it. The leaders of the Durham Miners' Association dated the county's resurgence from the 1870s, date of their own foundation; the coalfield Cooperators dated it from the 1850s and 1860s; the Methodists dated it from the 1830s and 1840s. All had their histories and photographs to attest: of bad old times when coalowners controlled the villages and pitmen were denied their independence; of good new times when premises, halls, schools, branches, officials and members, bands and banners lined up to show their amelioration, to witness their achievement. On the miners' banners, every message was one of salvation. Local and regional visions were flanked by national and international ones. It wasn't just that the county looked different from the miners' side; more, it was a miners' county. For Greenside Lodge banner, there was the pit nationalised, 'for the People by the People'; for Marsden Lodge banner, there was nearby Marsden Rock jutting into the sea, like the people, 'Firm as a Rock'.

A true People demanded a true language. The emergence of the dialect as a regional badge served to consolidate the working-class claim. Certainly, the written dialect was as contrived a device as The People who were supposed to speak it. Both were a performance, but what is crucial here is that if the dialect was construed as regional and open to all, its true guardians were the working class. The Trade may have been presented as a community of interests, The People as a community of history and the dialect as a community of speech, but in each case it was the other classes who were invited to join the workers – even if only for 'a try' – and not the other way round. In the new Board schoolrooms, the children were being told that their way of speaking was slovenly while outside, quite astonishingly, there was a regional identity which celebrated their speech and not the teacher's. Anyone intent on a popular audience could use the dialect and adapt it. The music hall thundered out its own versions of regional identity every bit as effectively as did the labour movement, the civic dignitaries or the antiquarians. In many cases, the various strands intertwined. What the antiquarians thought was folk culture was often popular culture, what the civic dignitaries thought was popular culture was sometimes class culture and what the socialists thought was class culture could be something much older – but in the end it didn't matter. By 1914, the North-East was established as a region where the working-class presence was pre-eminent. Even the New Northumbrians had to break their rural reverie and find a place for 'Labour' and 'Industry'. Even today, a middle-class Geordie sounds wrong. If this was patriotism, it was very different from the national variety. Made rich by its labour and known by its industry, the North-East was a people's region.

'Labour' and 'Industry' as categories of response were joined from the 1920s by a third category, 'Decline'. From the outside, some of this decline was assigned to capitalism as 'Industry', usually in terms of a blighted landscape. Those innovating entrepreneurs of yesteryear were less in evidence, it is true, but as individuals it was presumed they could look after themselves. The real shock of decline was addressed to 'Labour'. After half a century of painting and photographing workers as 'Labour' at work or in places of work, and understanding the North-East as a people's place, suddenly workers were shorn of their power. Now unemployed, and vulnerable, they were human again – but hardly men. Now denied their trade, they might remain The People, or, as with Priestley, the *true* People – but the buoyancy was gone. Priestley was sympathetic but not confident. He said he didn't like the dialect. And anyway, what sort of true People could need help from a Tory government in the South? Even in more prosperous times when work returned, 'Decline', as measured against old ways of seeing 'Labour' and 'Industry', lingered still. In June 1976, the magazine *19* could refer to 'Decline' almost as a regional custom: 'Traditionally it has been the area of industrial decline . . .', a grim trait which still did not debar the North-East from being 'well worth a visit'.

From the inside, for a long time the labour movement tarried with all three responses. After all, they were interdependent, and the notion of wasted 'Labour' or idle 'Industry' was a useful strategy in attracting attention to the region's problems. After 1945, the very idea of the North-East as a 'special' or a 'deprived' region gave the male response new life in a series of central government regional policies. However, today the strategy no longer holds. In the face of more expert, more ubiquitous image-making competitors from outside, and the erosion of its skilled, manual working base from within, the capacity of the labour movement to represent the region in these male categories has gone. Of course, the Labour-Industry-Decline formulation was always a selection of men by men, but that is not to say that its voice was not authentic. Built on masculine pride, the voice could command confidence well into the 1980s. Graham Myers was a fitter at Smith's Shipbuilders, Middlesbrough:

> The work itself, I've always enjoyed it – enjoyed the idea of building a ship. I think a ship is probably the best thing you could build as far as job satisfaction goes. You build a ship and it actually moves. You go on trials with them and then they sail out at the end, you think you've done something towards that. The job I've got now I'm going to be building transformers for microwave ovens but there's no way on this earth that I'm going to walk into a shop that sells microwave ovens and say 'Oh, I helped to build them'. It's just not the same, it's a job, it pays your wages and that's it. Whereas this, you could bring the wife or the girlfriend or your mother or somebody down to the shipyard and say 'Look, this is what we do' and actually get a feeling of pride. I would never take somebody round a factory and show them transformers, because it's nothing.
>
> (Macdonald and Tabner, *Smith's Docks*, 1989)

Graham Myers used to be a shipbuilder. In the North-East, so many people and places *used to be* that the region is hardly discussed without reference to what went before. Men name themselves by occupation – a fitter 'by trade' – even when no longer in that occupation. Coping with this sense of loss has turned the region into a company of historians, and affiliation is demanded early.

That landscape which first signified the region as a labour region – cranes, hulls, factory chimneys, pit winding gear – has all but vanished. The day is not far off when only the Tyne Bridge will remain as an example of this landscape. Industrial aesthetics were never easy or clean, but they did possess a strong, masculine resonance. And, as in the 1930s, it has not been possible in recent times to dissociate obsolete structures from the men who worked in them. In the 1970s, commercial interests were not slow to illustrate 'Geordie' as a fool, a caricature of obsolescent masculinity. Only an older, more generous, popular tradition of ironic humour, ranging from Bob Cranky in the nineteenth century to Bobby Thompson in the twentieth, saved this cloth-capped moron from the rejection he deserved. The Royal Academy showed interest in obsolescence too, especially when it promised new bait for artistic sensibilities. L. S. Lowry was attracted by the North-East's 'peculiar character and atmosphere'. His depiction of the region was drawn to dereliction, loss and oddity. Similarly, Sirkka-Liisa Konttinen's photography was fated by a sense of what Byker had been, compared to what it was when she lived there. Konttinen's Byker is desolate and old, even when it is teeming and young. Along with Killip's collection *In Flagrante*, her photography gets inside but nevertheless works within a tradition of obsolescence and sadness. Plater, Chaplin and Glasgow's *Close The Coalhouse Door*, a drama performed at the Newcastle Playhouse between 1968 and 1969, was undoubtedly the greatest last shout of a masculine North-East. Written by insiders, their call was to close the door on the past ('There's blood inside'), but everything in the play sang of holding on to what was worth having.

The time is not yet ripe for the old patrimony of Labour-Industry-Decline to be ditched. Yet, no matter how the convenion develops, in reality the male response has gone and is not likely to come back. For those following the generation born in the 1940s, such a culture will be only hearsay. No regional identity which lives on hearsay can have a future. Nor does it deserve to.

SELLING PLACES

Selling places has become big business. After a lifetime of being told in the schoolbooks that regional personality follows culture as culture follows geographical settlement, the means now exist to sell regional personalities almost before their culture exists. This representation of places for money in the hope of inward investment or tourism some academics call 'the commoditisation of culture'. The growth of mass communication, local government bureaucracy and a national grid for energy supply have each played a key part. Thus, Glasgow became the 1990 European City of Culture by a decision of the European Cultural Affairs Committee of the European Commission. The publicity was smart and plentiful. Hopes for new investment in the region were high. Scottish coal no longer mattered. The thing was invented in Brussels, designed in Glasgow and broadcast to the world. It can only be a question of time before Newcastle too becomes a City of Something.

The selling of places raises vital questions about the representation of regions. Advertising professionals are expert in representing the best bits, the golden stones, the tourist-commercial square miles. As the Northern Rock Building Society showed when they wanted to sell a bank account, quayside Newcastle can look stylish when filmed at 4:20 a.m., in grainy black and white, in sixty seconds of enigmatic shadow. Equally, the heritage professionals can reinterpret historical meanings on a scale previously unimagined, all for the price of a museum, with customers. Image-makers understand at least this much: that in an image-glutted market, each place has to be construed as different from other places, and, in the making of each uniqueness, history, or 'heritage', matters. In 1973, 'Northumbria' was reborn yet again, this time in Grosvenor Crescent, SW1. P&A Management Consultants were hired to advise on tourism. First, they laid out the North-East as an economic audit. Second, they fiddled with the history and geography to suggest Durham City as regional capital, or 'product leader'. Third, they concluded that something they called 'history' was the region's best asset. Five years later, the Northumbrian Tourist Board reported on what had been learned. Professor Archer loaned academic respectability to the computation of what an invented place earned and spent. In 1978, earnings from tourism were estimated at £70m: roughly forty per cent had come from holidaymakers, 'but of even greater significance' the rest had come from business conferences and socioeconomic category A and B visitors. The Director called for 'aggressive marketing' among those categories. No wonder Mr Bert Sharples of Hartlepool felt the odds were stacked against him.

Who sells what to whom and for how much? In the business of representation, places are sold competitively, one place against another, for high rewards. The Nissan car company had to be persuaded that Sunderland was superior to rival contenders and there was more to that than greenfield sites, labour costs and single-union deals. Nowadays, the Northern Development Company and the Urban Development Corporations are the leading sellers, but as long ago as 1967 Graham Turner realised that public relations was 'considered to be a prerequisite for luring Southern executives to the area'; 'this is one part of the North where you feel ceaselessly worked upon'.

The image market represents the region to the nation, and the region to itself. It seeks to affect expectations, to reconstruct history, to reinterpret experience, to change meanings and to switch meanings according to the groups targeted. The market even seeks to redraw and rename the region's space. South Shields used to bid welcome to careful drivers. Now the drivers are welcomed to 'Catherine Cookson Country'. Of course, cultural manipulation is not new. What is new is its ubiquity and the speed, resource and skill with which it is carried out. Often, the new cultural gerrymanderers wield their power quite shamelessly. Competing or contradictory *local* meanings are bulldozed, sometimes literally so, once the developers move in. While Sunderland's last shipyard was being torn apart for the scrapheap, 'the local business community' was promoting Wearside 'as the Advanced Manufacturing Centre of the North'. In their full-page advert, 'Positive thinking in the land of light', the Chief Executive of Sunderland Polytechnic was featured to show how someone who was born in Kent could choose to live 'close to Sunderland'. Why man, she even convinced her brother, 'a confirmed Londoner', to come up over Christmas and see 'one of the best pantomimes in the country ...'. He wouldn't have had to look far.

We have referred to places being sold, but everyone knows that real regions are not for sale and that real cultures are not commodities. To sell a region is to sell a culture, yet 'culture' is an elusive article. It is not a thing, more a set of relationships and, before 'it' can be commoditised, 'it' has to be represented in ways which are at least recognisable to those who constitute those relationships.

Unlike other commodities, therefore, regional culture as a commodity has to be 'bought' first by those who in some sense possess it already. Clever selling does this, not so much in words but in photography. Learning from the surrealists in the 1930s, professional photographers made all subjects valid. Poor people became as valid as rich people, ordinary things as valid as special things. Photojournalism encouraged the trend, a trend which Susan Sontag in *On Photography* (1979) saw as an 'uncompromisingly egalitarian attitude toward subject matter'. This democratic impression was perfectly suited to mass advertising. Whether it be the Chief Executive of Sunderland Polytechnic or a bunch of sausages, selling has learned the art of the everyday. Images of what we want to be, or possess, are simultaneously images of what we see in ourselves, or possess in some sense already. By consuming, the region appears to be speaking for itself. In its extreme form, selling can claim that the real region exists through what it consumes. The North-East buys relatively little electrical equipment and eats a lot of rice pudding. So what? Marketing man Ellison Allan had the answer:

> On closer scrutiny, however ... these findings ... group themselves more or less naturally ... into larger clusters ... each of which exemplifies some broader theme of behaviour ... These clusters ... prove to stand in a meaningful relationship to one another and gradually coalesce into a single, logically consistent whole. This whole, therefore, we may legitimately term the regional 'personality'.
>
> (*British Tastes*, 1968)

DEFENDING THE CULTURE

The North-East is less able to defend itself from misrepresentation. Local capital is marginal to the regional economy and cannot affect the directions the region might take. Lord Armstrong was a great international capitalist, but he was never anonymous or absent from the region. It mattered to him how he and his business were seen by Tyneside in a way that it does not matter to national and transnational corporations. Local intellectual capital is weaker too. All that middle-class intellectual effort which identified the region as a 'Northumbria' both ancient and modern has diminished in influence. Enthusiasts still walk and look and imagine, but their attachments are fewer and their power to identify the region is weaker. The Newcastle Literary and Philosophical Society, to give just one example, is no longer the bearer of higher education in the city. Nor is the region's labour movement as able as it was to express a distinctive view. Through this movement in all its rich associational life, from sports clubs to cooperative societies to trade unions, the working classes were better able to represent themselves in terms of labour power, skill, cultural enterprise, organisational achievement and a dense community presence. Today, the skills are less widespread, less controlled, less defended; the cultural enterprise has to cope with more powerful, private or state, formations; the political movements' institutional and ideological coherence hardly exists; and the communities, or many of them, have been razed to the ground, redeveloped, rehoused or, as in the 1984-5 miners' strike, beaten into submission. At times, it seems that only the dialect remains strong.

The North-East has its bards, of course. Some of them appear in this volume. Part of their problem, as Alan Plater says, lies in keeping as short a distance as possible between them and their subjects. Those who stayed in their community hardly needed to be reminded. For Jimmy Forsyth, there was little choice. Unemployed and dependent on benefit, Forsyth's most valuable possession was his bus pass. And his photograph collection – a named and dated gallery of people and places in the Scotswood Road area of Newcastle, a record of a working-class community before and while the planners moved in. Forsyth's subjects look pleased to be snapped (see Figure 1.4). Often they asked to be photographed, and bought and showed the prints afterwards: 'They were waiting to hear about moving and wanted a picture of themselves with the old house to remember it by.'

Norman Cornish is another who stayed, to paint. After thirty-three years working in the pits of South Durham, Cornish, with the Ashington painters, found his tutors in adult education and his subjects round the corner. His pictures centre on the pub, the street and the pit. Working with what he knew best, it was in these places that Cornish found breadth in depth – robust figures of 'peasant' strength and rootedness in a European naturalist tradition, but also a local intimacy which bound them one to another and all to their place. For the problem of distance is never just a matter of staying physically near. Affiliation is as important as distance. In

FIGURE 1.4: 'Forsyth's subjects look pleased to be snapped.' *Girl against front door* (1958), Photograph: courtesy of Jimmy Forsyth and West Newcastle Local Studies Centre (from *Scotswood Road*, Bloodaxe Books, 1986).

Catherine Cookson's case, the problem of distance/affiliation is particularly tense. First, before she was a writer, there was a conscious decision to leave the North-East and forget it. Then, when her need to affiliate became urgent, and with it the impulse to write, she was far away and outside the obvious affiliations. As a Geordie, Cookson was drawn to her region. As a woman, the region's masculine identity was not open to her in the way it was open to the men. As such, Catherine Cookson is a paradox. She is the North-East's most famous writer, a woman whose name is synonymous with the region itself, yet she is not a regional writer. From the outside, she had to find her own ways of telling. In the event, these ways were women's ways. Her stories are set in the North-East, but it is not the region which matters; they could be just about anywhere. Unlike Cookson, Sid Chaplin was at ease with his region. Although his writing moved him away from his native Durham, he retained an artistry bent on keeping in touch with its storytellers. By staying near, Forsyth, Cornish and Chaplin ran less risk of patronage than did Jack Common, who left. Yet, as working-class men, they all shared the possibility of affiliation. By leaving, Cookson should have been patronised but was not. A woman writing in a 'woman's genre', she was left alone with a form, 'romance', that was not considered worthy of patronage.

When our artists leave, they run the risk of patronage. When they stay, they run the risk of recognition as simple 'regional' folk. If they are women, the problem is more difficult still. Yet, however one looks at it, for as long as the North-East is dependent upon the enlarged sympathy of other, more powerful places, there is no easy answer. In the meantime, for our bards and remembrancers, part of the solution to the problem of defending the culture is to remember there's a problem.

And the problem is not only on the inside. All of the bards considered here have tried to depict, and forge, a common culture. That has been one of their defences of it. Now, as we have seen, the idea of culture is increasingly subject to wilful misrepresentation. Most insidiously, it is becoming the acceptable face of distinction. Class distinction is no longer polite. Race and gender distinctions are formally unacceptable. What we are told we inhabit today, in all our differentness, are 'cultures' fixed and forever – or at least forever fixed outside the grasp of those who are deemed to live them. This brand of multiculturalism sees 'Geordieland' as a cultural ghetto hiding its inequality behind something called its character, speaking colourfully but unintelligibly behind something called its accent. This is the old patronage made glossy. As ever, the defenders of the culture cannot afford to be beguiled. If the region's culture has already been made, and cannot change, then there is nothing to defend but the past. We have to defend the future too.

In conclusion, with an old, masculine view of the North-East receding, with new representations flowing fast from those whose aim is consumption rather than truth, with a region less able to represent itself on a scale which can compete with the image-makers, and in a society whose 'cultures' are becoming the fashionable expressions for stasis and inequality, it might seem that the full cultural franchise of the region is a distant prospect. But this is not necessarily so. Cultural *origins* are one thing, cultural *destinations* another. The former are easier to locate, and currently depressing. The latter are more difficult to trace, and less predictable. English history is not short of examples of the failure of the powerful to represent others in ways originally intended. The origins of state schooling did not find their destination in a docile people, nor did the origins of evangelical religion find their destination in saved and submissive congregations. The regional need for an identity which is appropriate, in terms of what Kevin Lynch in his *Image of the City* (1960) called 'legibility', 'imageability', 'visibility', will find its own path.

'Do we exist? What proof do we have? . . . When did we become a people? When did we stop being one? Or are we in the process of becoming one?' Edward Said's questions can be addressed to the Geordies also. If the North-East wants to save itself and secure a future, it will have to claim the right to its own representation. In a centralised and secretive British constitution, where one political party takes the region for granted and the other writes it off, this must involve devolution, and not just devolution from London. In a regionally devolving Europe, this could mean that the region becomes part of a European North-West as well as an English North-East. And this representation will have to be cultural as well as political, for only by telling its own stories will the region get a sense of the whole, and only by making sense of the whole will it know what to represent. Art is socially useful. However one tries to measure its achievement, it is *the doing* which helps people to see where they are and what they value. This chapter has concentrated on painting and writing, but there are other forms. Through music, drama, poetry and cinema, the people of the North-East could claim their right to be in a wider world – a right not often heard from either the Minister for the Arts (who?) or the Shadow Minister for the Arts (who again?).

TELLING OUR OWN STORIES

In December 1988, the government minister declared that the British Shipbuilders' yards at Austin & Pickersgill's, Sunderland, would close unless a private buyer could be found. Two buyers, one Greek and one German, were found. Both wanted to expand, the

FIGURE 1.5: 'In December 1988, the government minister declared that the British Shipbuilders' yards at Austin & Pickersgill's, Sunderland, would close unless a private buyer could be found. Two buyers, one Greek and one German, were found. Both wanted to expand, the new orders would be for their own shipping lines, and neither buyer required subsidies. In July 1989, the government turned down the offers.' *Prime Minister at Austin & Pickersgill's*, to launch the 123rd SD14 'United Effort' cargo vessel (12 March 1982), Photograph: Newcastle upon Tyne Libraries and Arts (© Newcastle Chronicle and Journal Ltd).

new orders would be for their own shipping lines, and neither buyer required subsidies.

In July 1989, the government turned down the offers (see Figure 1.5). In a ruling which contradicted the prime minister's deepest convictions – free markets and national sovereignty – her old friend Sir Leon Brittan at the European Commission decided that, after a secret deal done with the British Government, it was not possible to sell the yards for shipbuilding without threatening the aid package intended for Sunderland. The sting was this: for years, these ship-builders had been criticised for living off subsidies; for this, they had been slandered, threatened, run down; but now that they could compete without subsidy, they could not, *for fear of losing a subsidy.*

Between January and July 1986, the poet Tom Pickard had been
writer in residence at the yards. In *We Make Ships*, he recorded the
conversations of the welders' cabin. Their talk revealed an old class
masculinity fighting to survive. The odds were impossible, even for
men who thought they were fighters. British shipowners did not
build British, the government stuck to free-market theories, the
world market was depressed, global competition was subsidised,
every order was the subject of managerial brinkmanship, every job
had to be negotiated, or shared, with other trades, other unions,
and protected from outside contractors, cowboy firms, those who
had taken redundancy money but come back, the unemployed, the
lump. At the top was a state corporation that set yard against yard,
river against river, and a local management intent upon casuali-
sation and subcontracting. Hovering above were the asset-strip-
pers, the buyout teams, the speculators who wanted the riverbank
but not its skills. One day, the men in the cabin asked for some
songs from Pickard, the 'wierdo-poet':

Pickard:	Is that a commission? I think you should put a resolution to your union that you have a permanent...
Tony:	Writer! And a singer!
Pickard:	In every yard! Singer, artist, photographer...
Tony:	Like Robin Hood had, he had his own fucking...
Paul:	Minstrels!
Tony:	What did he call them?
Paul:	Minstrels.
Tony:	I know that, I mean his name, Robin Hood's minstrels. Alan Adair, wasn't it?
Pickard:	That's what the upper class has.

This is the Pickard Clause: we remember, therefore we are.
Whether welder, shop assistant, secretary, teacher or TV producer, it is worth its place in anyone's bargain. Much of this book
deals in facts, but the biggest fact of all, the region's sense of self, is a
fiction. Fiction makes reality keener, and the closer the better. If the
North-East is to survive into another century, it must be free to
make its own stories, stories that can be given back to temper shape
and substance. All the authors of *Geordies* hope that these stories
will do just that.

CHAPTER TWO

What Sort of Future?

DAVID BYRNE

THERE IS NO SINGLE ANSWER to the question in the title. Rather, there are a range of possibilities from which a choice has to be made. *It is not a matter of what will happen but of what will be made to happen.* And the range of choices is constrained. What has happened sets a limit on what can be made to happen.

We begin by setting the context, dealing with what the North-East has been in terms of industrial and social history and in terms of the popular consciousness created out of the experience of that history by generations of working-class people. The question 'what sort of future?' is about where we are going. We need to begin by remembering where we are coming from. This is particularly important because it is collective experience which sets social objectives. It is easy to identify the overwhelmingly collectivist and socialist objectives of the people of the Northern region. However easy that identification is, it is also absolutely necessary to establish because the present economic and political trends run directly counter to those objectives.

We go on to deal with those trends, with what will happen if things go on as they are. If the present quasi-colonial dominance of the North-East by an anti-collectivist central government, with no electoral base in the region, is allowed to continue, then not only will the result be a nasty, greedy, divided society in this region, but also the actual possibilities for development in a different direction will be pre-empted. We probably have from now until the year 2000 to do something about getting things right. After that, it will be much harder.

Finally, we look at what might be, at the kind of future which we might create between now and about 2050 – when the children of the author's generation will be as old as our parents are now – if the people of the North-East manage to get control over their own lives and collective destiny. We will pay particular attention to the political mechanisms which will be necessary for the acquisition of such control, for the giving to citizens of a democratic region the right to make their world as they want, and to make their own mistakes in getting to that world if they so desire.

FROM THE HEIGHTS TO THE DEPTHS AND UP AGAIN AND DOWN AGAIN

In his review of the region's history conducted for the 1970 Durham meeting of the British Association for the Advancement of Science, W. M. Hughes commented that:

> It is perhaps hard for us to realise after the years of the interwar depression that for sixty years before 1914 the Durham (and North-umberland) pitmen and the shipyard workers of the Tyne and Wear were among the most highly paid workers in the world outside the USA ... The decline into the poverty of the interwar years was from the heights to the depths.

This observation is exactly right, but we need to expand on it, to understand what factors had led to the situation in 1914 and what sort of world they had created. The North-East is one of the birthplaces of industrial capitalism and of the industrial working class. It shares with west central Scotland that combination of mining and engineering capitalism which was so crucial in the development of the technological basis of much of our sort of society. It also shares with west central Scotland the derivation of its working class from a mixture of indigenous and immigrant strands and the welding together of these strands into a particularly cohesive, self-conscious and active proletariat which played no small part in forcing the technological developments of late-nineteenth- and early-twentieth-century capitalism. What it does not share with Scotland is the poisonous impact of religious sectarianism.

To summarise the region's economic and social development: the mining of coal from the Middle Ages onwards provided the region with a very early capitalist and proletarian society which, taken together with the availability of substantial capital generated from modernised agriculture in the late eighteenth century, was well placed to take off on an enormous scale at the beginning of the nineteenth century. The population of the region increased from 645,000 in 1801 to 3,000,000 in 1921, at which level it has remained, being estimated at 3,077,000 in 1989.

The basis of this growth was a linked series of developments. First, the coal trade expanded with the development of railways, a North-Eastern invention, which permitted the exploitation of reserves further from river transport. This coal was brought to the rivers for shipment, which led to enormous development of the ports – the River Tyne was converted, in the words of the Tyne Improvement Commission's manager in the 1920s, from a muddy ditch to one of the world's great harbours – and of the shipping industry. This in turn led to developments in marine engineering, from which was derived a system of power-generation engineering, and more recently a complex of offshore production for oil extraction. The demand for iron and steel led to the creation of an iron industry, and cheap coal was the basis of a chemical industry, in the years before 1914 located on the Tyne as well as on the Tees. The system was integrated in terms of industrial and finance capital, and in terms of the knowledge and skill base which underpinned it.

This system of production required labour, and the labour had to be reproduced. The pattern of settlements in the North-East today derives from that developed to house the people who worked in this system. It was flung together, particularly between 1860 and 1914, which were the years of greatest immigration. What was created, especially after 1860, was not rubbish. The working class was too well paid and too well organised to accept rubbish. However, the North-East's urban industrialism was created as a rush job on the back of older systems. Until very recently, one of the major problems of social policy in the region had been the rectification of the deficiencies created by that period of rushed industrialisation and urbanisation. Now one of the problems is the rectification of the problems created by those very housing and planning policies directed at rectifying the earlier problems! Nevertheless, until the collapse of 1921, the problems were problems of growth. The North-East was an industrial hellhole, but it was a prospering industrial hellhole with a particularly self-confident and well-organised industrial working class.

FIGURE 2.1: 'Jarrow, for example, plunged from the heights of high-waged shipyard employment to the depths of over seventy per cent unemployment.' *Jarrow March* (1936), Photograph: South Tyneside Libraries.

The interwar structural decline of the region changed all that. H. A. Mess's statistical profile of *Industrial Tyneside* (1928) and J. B. Priestley's impressionistic account in *English Journey* (1934), in their different ways, both described a society in which the transition from prosperity to poverty had occurred so suddenly that the region was faced with the worst aspects of both situations. This was particularly evident in housing and urban conditions. The congestion created by industrial growth remained without the high real wages which had attracted the workers in the first place. Jarrow, for example, plunged from the heights of high-waged shipyard employment to the depths of over seventy per cent unemployment (see Figure 2.1), and had some of the worst urban conditions in the UK and the highest TB rate in England.

The proposals for regional development which were organised around the reports of the Special Areas Commissioners in the 1930s were an interesting and fruitful combination of macroeconomic industrial strategy and Keynesian social strategy. The industrial strategy was that of diversification of the economic base through the encouragement of new industrial sectors based on industrial estates. Team Valley in Gateshead was one triumphant manifestation of this programme, but there are other large industrial estates throughout the North-East, and it is worth noting that it was at this time that the fate of industrial West Cumbria became administratively linked with the North-East. On the social side, the strategy was one of public expenditure on social and environmental developments, which was useful both in itself in rectifying past deficiencies and in stimulating the regional economy by the injection of wage-based expenditure. All public bodies were involved in this programme, but the major initiatives were associated with a new political form, the corporatist political organisations created by the Special Areas Commissioner in the form of appointed rather than elected bodies. These bodies were so constructed as to include representatives of the major interest groups – organised labour, industrial capitalism, landed interests and local government. The significance of this separation of economic development from direct democratic control by local government cannot be overstated.

During and after the war, the North-East's basic economy was revived. The heavy engineering and carboniferous capitalism of the region was changed remarkably little by the nationalisation of coal and rail, and prospered under the conditions of postwar shortages of world productive capacity. Indeed, the general level of economic activity was massively increased by the bringing of more and more married women into productive employment. The peak of the North-East as an industrial zone was in the late 1950s and early 1960s, with enormous male and female workforces in manufacturing and still a very large male workforce in coalmining. During this period, there was some industrial diversification, particularly with the development of clothing and electrical goods.

The first real postwar crisis came in the early 1960s, when a change in the availability of energy sources led to a shift in fuel policy from coal towards oil. The National Coal Board, which had pursued a policy of maximising production more or less regardless of cost, was forced to change almost overnight to a profit-led system. Under the direction of Lord Robens, this led to a large programme of pit closures. Between 1957 and 1974, the North-East lost over 100,000 mining jobs from a total of 150,000.

This structural change in the region's economic base was recognised as being of crucial national political significance. The prime minister, Harold Macmillan, formerly MP for Stockton during the Depression, was fully prepared to initiate the kind of interventionist programme for which he had argued from the Tory left at that time, and Labour continued it in the 1960s. The programme, associated with Hailsham's 'cloth cap' visit in his capacity as Minister for the North-East, was a larger-scale version of the approaches of the 1930s. It combined investment in social and economic infrastructure with an incentive-led form of indicative planning designed to attract new manufacturing development.

This period saw very real successes. The programme of infrastructure developments continued through the 1960s and 1970s, and to a very considerable degree rectified the North-East's social deficits as compared with the UK as a whole. This was particularly true for housing, where the North-East was converted from the worst-housed region in England into one of the best. Transport infrastructure was also much improved, and a start was made on redressing health deficits through the operation of the RAWP mechanism by which the allocation of health resources was related to health needs in the NHS. The significant omission was in higher education, where the North-East did not receive a new university and Teesside was left as the largest UK conurbation without one.

Industrial development was also successful in the short term. The enormous job losses in mining were compensated for by new manufacturing employment. However, the new plants were very much part of the new social organisation of capitalist production. They are usually referred to as 'branch plants', although recent discussion about the political economy of space (see Massey 1985) suggests that this term is inappropriate. What matters is the spatial separation of functions of strategic management, research and development from the site of actual production. The popular description of much of the industrial development of this era as involving the importation of 'headless chickens' conveys the idea very well. And this strategy has not been abandoned, particularly in relation to Japanese capital. Nissan at Washington is a classic headless chicken. Developments since the election of a Conservative government in 1979 have taken a generally different direction.

Before proceeding to a discussion of the economic and social experiences of the North-East under Mrs Thatcher, we need to consider the decline of Conservative politics in this region, albeit from a low starting point. In the elections which were held for the new Tyne and Wear Metropolitan Districts in 1973, the Conservatives won over a third of the seats contested and were, together with their 'Progressive' allies in South Tyneside, the leading opposition in every district. In elections held under the Labour Government between 1974 and 1979, they increased their number of seats held and had serious hopes of winning control in Newcastle and North Tyneside. Since 1979 and the advent of Mrs Thatcher, however, they have steadily lost seats to the point where, in 1991, they held only one seat in Gateshead and two, with a 'Progressive' ally, in South Tyneside. Overall, in 1991 they held only ten per cent of Tyne and Wear District seats and were not even the official opposition in Gateshead and Newcastle, having been replaced by the Liberal Democrats. Labour held two thirds of Tyne and Wear seats in 1973. In 1991, they held eighty per cent of all seats. Of course, this is in part a reflection of the impact of the first-past-the-post system when there are three parties in contention, but it also reflects the elimination of Conservatism as a serious political force in Tyne and Wear politics. This makes it very difficult for a Conservative central administration to have any legitimate voice in local politics, because it has no real local representation. Perhaps the real point of contrast is not 1973 but the situation as it was in the 1960s and early 1970s when Conservatives and their allies at various times controlled the county boroughs of Newcastle, Sunderland and South Shields, and Gateshead was only retained under Labour control by the Aldermen, with the majority of elected councillors being Conservative. In these inner urban areas, the Conservatives in 1991 had about five per cent of all seats.

The situation with parliamentary seats is almost as dramatic. Prior to the 1992 general election, the only seat held by the Conservatives in Tyne and Wear was Tynemouth, with a minority of votes cast and a majority over Labour of some 2,000. The Conservatives have in the past held the seats which correspond to the present Newcastle Central, Newcastle East and Sunderland South. They have no prospect whatsoever of winning these seats today. The North-East as a whole, and Tyne and Wear in particular, has been marginalised in the UK electoral system. The Conservatives regard it as a dead loss and Labour as a foregone conclusion – in the latter case in sharp contrast with urban Scotland, where there is an ever-present threat from the Nationalists.

THE NORTH-EAST UNDER MRS THATCHER

The election of a 'New Right' Conservative administration in 1979 had very profound effects for the region, which took several forms. First, the pursuit of a monetarist, macroeconomic strategy, favouring finance capital at the expense of industrial capital, took the particular form of a grossly overvalued pound in the early 1980s, and contributed to the general decline of UK manufacturing industry across a range of sectors and to massive industrial job losses in the North-East as in all industrial regions. Conservative macroeconomic policy since 1979 has squandered the profits of North Sea oil. Far from being used as the basis of a modernising industrial strategy, oil revenues have underpinned an actively hostile approach towards the manufacturing base.

A particular aspect of this general hostility has had massive significance for the North-East. As Hudson demonstrated in *Wrecking a Region* (1989), the active destruction of nationalised industries by Conservative-appointed management, in association with a hostile ministerial regime at the Departments of Energy and Industry (see Figure 2.2), has eliminated enormous numbers of jobs in what were the nationalised sectors of coal, iron and steel, and shipbuilding. These job losses were of course in large part a specific consequence of general economic policy, but they also originated in explicit political hostility to trade-union power in the UK economy. The Conservatives were out to break the organised working class, both by legislative attacks on effective capacity for industrial action and by the destruction of the industrial basis of organisation itself. Managers representing industrial capital may have been keen to regain the right to manage, and they certainly have regained it to a considerable degree in what is left of the industrial base. However, they have done so by means of supporting a programme of cutting off noses to spite faces. This is particularly the case with shipbuilding, where Sunderland Shipbuilders was closed in the face of unequivocal evidence of its potential profitability in the context of a developing world shortage of merchant shipbuilding capacity (see Figure 2.3). Here, the decent trade unionism of the North-East was sacrificed to maintain a bastion of sectarianism in Belfast through a secret deal with the EEC Commission. Sunderland became a Jarrow of the 1990s. Another town has been murdered.

FIGURE 2.2: '... the active destruction of nationalised industries by Conservative-appointed management, in association with a hostile ministerial regime at the Departments of Energy and Industry...' *Consett Steelworks* (1983), Photograph: Newcastle upon Tyne Libraries and Arts (© Newcastle Chronicle and Journal Ltd).

The response of the North-East's political elites to these developments has been strangely muted. The corporatist collaborators of regional TUC officials, Labour councillors, CBI-orientated industrialists and traditional landowners have not welcomed the Thatcher approach, but have proved singularly incapable of framing any very coherent opposition to it. The main reason for this, in the view of this author, is the absence of serious opposition from the left, and in particular from the unofficial organisations of the working class. In the North-East, the only serious, autonomous, working-class organisation in the postwar years took the form of industrial syndicalism by shop stewards, a movement which was weakened by developments from 1979 onwards. It is important to recognise, however, that the weakening began before the election of Mrs Thatcher. Perhaps the high point of the syndicalist project of workers' control in relation to formal politics was the passing of the

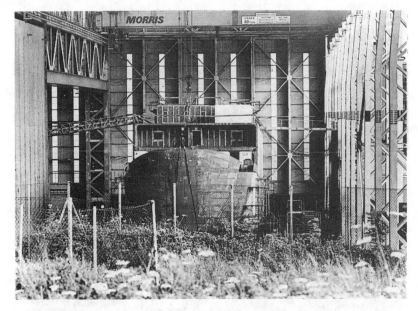

FIGURE 2.3: '... closed in the face of unequivocal evidence of its potential profitability in the context of a developing world shortage of merchant ship-building capacity.' *North-East Shipbuilders, Sunderland* (1987), Photograph: Newcastle upon Tyne Libraries and Arts (© Newcastle Chronicle and Journal Ltd).

1975 Industry Act, with its apparent commitment to workers' participation in industrial planning. The two Tyneside Community Development Projects, together with the Tyneside Conference of Shop Stewards, established the Trade Union Studies Unit in Newcastle to act as a servicing agency for the unofficial movement in such planning. The abandonment of this programme by the Labour government after the intervention of the International Monetary Fund in 1975 was the crucial turning point away from this sort of strategy. The corporatist regional institutions resumed their importance.

Potentially, at least, struggles in production are not the only source of pressure from below. There is also the possibility of struggles over community. The Community Development Projects were very committed to such action, and drew on the extremely important previous experiences of the National Unemployed Workers Movement in the 1930s and of housing struggles in the years before the First World War, but developments since the mid1970s have been complicated by the state's use of co-optive community work organised by poverty professionals. Thus there has not been a major pressure on the central establishment from autonomous organisations in either production or community-building. This is not to say that there is not potential for such pressure.

So far, the account of developments in the economic base has been presented in terms of competing national economic strategies, of a Conservative government which has favoured financial, and Southern, capital at the expense of Northern manufacturing, and of a political strategy of eliminating the power of labour organised at the point of production. This is all true, but it is useful to think about developments using a different vocabulary, the 'p' words of post-modernism, post-industrialism and post-modernisation, all of which are essentially cultural in character.

The term 'post-modern' originates in discussions of art, literature and architecture, but has been taken more generally to describe a society in which organised capitalism has become frag-mented and society is being progressively differentiated. Of par-ticular significance is the emergence, or creation, of a dispossessed underclass surplus to the requirements of a very different employ-ment system, and dependent for its existence on state benefits. One aspect of the post-modern is the notion that advanced societies are becoming 'post-industrial'. This has a range of meanings. In its most extreme form, the term expresses the notion that the import-ant product of advanced capitalist societies is not commodities, things which are used either directly as consumer goods or as capital goods to make other things, but information. In such societies, financial services have a particularly privileged place. Of course, improvements in labour productivity in advanced capi-talism mean that just as many commodities may be produced by a far smaller labour force. Deindustrialisation may be relative in that industrial productivity remains as high, or even increases, while the proportion of the workforce employed in industry reduces, or it may be absolute in that industrial production declines in formerly central industrial areas. This absolute decline is usually associated with a relocation of industrial production to other places – what is called the 'new international division of labour'. The North-East has been affected by both absolute and relative de-industrialisation. What industry that remains is more productive and employs fewer people to make more, but there has also been an absolute loss of industrial capacity. Between 1973 and 1988, the region lost 250,000 industrial jobs from an original total of 625,000. Between 1976 and 1987, industrial production declined by more than ten per cent in real terms.

Post-modernisation is a term used to describe a particular set of policies. The corporatist, regionalist strategy of reindustrialisation, a strategy which has long been the objective of regional elites drawn from local government, the trade unions, industrial capital and the landed nobility and gentry, was a policy of modernisation. It wanted to change the industrial structure to make it more competitive and innovative. Perhaps even more than this, it wanted to diversify it, so that the region would not be so vulnerable to market pressures in a restricted range of industrial sectors. It is worth remarking that the emphasis on diversification may have operated at the expense of modernisation of the existing industrial base. Diversification has led to a general emphasis on attracting branch plant investment and to a neglect of support for the existing core industrial structure. Witness the attention and support in all sorts of ways given in Sunderland by local government to the headless chicken of Nissan and the absence of attention to the historically immensely innovative shipbuilding sector. However, whatever the defects of the regionalist, corporatist strategy, it was, and remains so in the form of for example the Northern Development Company, industrially orientated. Indeed, in its highest development, in the form of the Northern Regional Strategy which derived from Labour's abortive National Plan of 1966, and as expressed in the Structure Plans which drew on that document, there was a clear realisation of the need to shift from attracting new industry at any price towards an industrial strategy which drew on the region's existing resources of both human and physical capital.

In contrast, recent developments have taken a very different turn. Despite some lip service to the creation of industrial jobs, they have been driven by a logic derived from short-term profit-making in land development and have even been instrumental in the destruction of existing industrial employment. Even more importantly, these recent developments, if allowed to take the course they propose, will pre-empt the possibility of future industrial investment which draws on traditional skills. The worst examples of this are provided by the two Urban Development Corporations. These bodies are directly appointed by the Secretary of State for the Environment, and have taken control of planning matters on and beside the three industrial rivers of Tyne, Wear and Tees. Their model is the discredited London Docklands Development Corporation which, at the cost of enormous public subsidy, has destroyed more permanent jobs than it has created and is primarily a vehicle for the yuppification of London's East End. It is now in crisis as the property market goes into a tailspin. The Tyne and Wear (Urban) Development Corporation and the Teesside UDC were just getting going as the rising property market, which was supposed to carry their activities, fell.

This is not to say that they have not got the potential to do a great deal of damage. This has already happened with the Tyne and Wear Development Corporation, which played a contributory role in preventing replacement shipbuilding development in Sunderland and has taken over one of Tyneside's prime river-fronting industrial sites for a yuppie village. Both UDCs have had appointed members with connections with the regional labour movement, including the Regional Secretary of the Transport and General Workers' Union who is also the Chair of the Regional Labour Party and combines these roles with appointed membership of a number of quangos. However, there is no discernible evidence of any impact by people like him on the policies of the UDCs. Indeed, they seem to have taken on the role of justifying UDC activity to their own labour movement.

This general post-industrial, post-modernising policy commitment is not, unfortunately, confined to the administrations of the UDCs and their local collaborators. It has also become characteristic of the orientation of much of elected local government. Newcastle City Council is run by a Labour group with a marked representation of local business and commercial interests which has constantly supported UDC-style developments. Durham County Council is another offender, with its ridiculous 'Land of the Prince Bishops' slogan. As so often happens, post-industrialism has become involved with a spurious assertion of the pre-industrial 'heritage' past. Cleveland County Council and North Tyneside MDC have been much more critical of such approaches, but there is a strong drift away from the clear industrial priorities. This is evident in the approaches being made to the new Unitary Development Plans which are replacing the Structure Plans, particularly in the Tyne and Wear conurbation. The abolition of the elected Tyne and Wear County Council has meant that crucial planning decisions are being taken away from the direct scrutiny of elected councillors as a whole. The emerging general orientation of such plans is towards breaches of green belts by mixed residential and 'business park' (for which read office) developments. The future is not just post-industrial, it is also post-urban.

What does all this add up to? The society which will be created if things are allowed to continue as they are is already with us in embryo. It will be divided. These divisions will take the form of a combination of economic role, lifestyle and area of residence – a three-way slicing where the boundaries between the divisions are imprecise and permeable. At one end will be the poor. The reality of life for these people will be that they are unemployed or under-employed. Manipulation of definitions and 'eligibility controls' have reduced the formally recorded number of unemployed people in the region, but we need to think of those who 'have not work and want it'. However, the distinction between unemployment and employment is not as simple as it used to be. One of the major contributions made by the Conservatives in their return to 'Victorian values' has been the reintroduction of 'underemployment' as an economic category. For the purposes of official statistics, a job is a job is a job, but from the point of view of the social commitment to full employment there is a very real distinction between a part-time job and a full-time job, and a similar distinction between regular employment and intermittent and irregular employment.

Many people in the North-East are underemployed. Many are also paid low wages. In important sectors, real wages have declined not just relatively but also absolutely with the weakening of trade-union resistance. The shift in core sectors from industry to services has been of crucial significance in increasing the incidence of low pay and underemployment. Those who depend on the combination of wages and benefits form a connection between the wholly benefit-dependent and 'ordinary working people'. The conditions of life of the wholly and partially benefit-dependent poor are perhaps better in the North-East than anywhere else in the UK because the socialist tradition of decent public services provides council housing which is usually adequate and often very good, and at the same time has managed to retain the remnants of a proper system of public transport. Even so, these people are much worse off than most. They form about forty per cent of all households in the region. They are variously council tenants, town-dwellers, and either old or young but not generally middle-aged. If things continue as they are, their lives will worsen with the reduction in public services in general and with the introduction of dual standards of provision in health and education.

The 'ordinary people' of the region improved their living standards under Mrs Thatcher. These are the people living in households which depend on wages derived from what remains of the industrial structure, from public services and from that part of the private services sector which does pay better. Most are owner occupiers and own a car. However, their lives, although comfortable, are insecure. If they lose a job, and many households depend for comfort on two jobs, they can fall down the scale very rapidly indeed. The poor, for them, function as a classic, disciplining, reserve army of labour, not as an irrelevant underclass, and they know it. They know it far better than people like them in the South know it, and they have systematically rejected Thatcherism in elections. They know their own interests and retain a sense of social solidarity with the poor which is one of the best aspects of the regional culture. This group contains about half the households in the region. If things continue as they are, about half of this group will become worse off. This poorer half will experience more unemployment with the continuing destruction of the industrial base and with cuts in public services and hence public-service employment. They too will suffer from the impact of dual-standard health and education provision.

Finally, there are the regional rich. This group contains about ten per cent of households in the region. The distinguishing characteristic is that they are not solely dependent on wages, or on the pensions which derive from wages, for their living. This group includes industrial capitalists, senior managers in both the public and private sectors, very highly remunerated professionals, land-owning farmers, richer tenant farmers and so on. This group has done very well under Mrs Thatcher, primarily in consequence of the elimination of higher rates of direct taxation, although the industrial managers and capitalists have suffered from the generally anti-industrial character of Conservative policies. If things go on as they are, most of them will do much better as owners of wealth in an unequal society. Yet, and somewhat to their credit, many of the members of this group are not keen on the divided future either. They prefer a more integrated, corporatist, generally prosperous society. It is the withdrawal from active commitment by these people which is one of the main explanations for the enormous decline in the Conservative Party in the North-East. They were quite happy with Macmillan-style 'one nation' Toryism, but found Mrs Thatcher deeply alienating. They are waiting to see what to make of Mr Major.

The projected future is as now, but worse. The 1980s have been another devil's decade, like the 1930s. Indeed, in terms of the deliberate malice of government, they have been rather worse. Is there an alternative? If there is, what are the preconditions of that alternative?

THE NORTH-EAST THAT THE PEOPLE WANT – AND HOW TO GET IT

The kind of society which people in the North-East want and vote for is quite easy to describe. It is more egalitarian, open, has a high level of public services, and is based on full employment in a successful and modern industrial structure. It looks very like Scandinavian social democracy, and the North-East with its three million people would make a very reasonably sized Scandinavian nation-state. This vision is not static. It is perfectly clear that environmental issues have a far higher profile than they did even ten years ago. Again, that is very like Scandinavia.

It must be emphasised that this sort of future is possible. It is a real alternative which draws on the existing character of the region's institutions and people, and which can provide the economic underpinning for social goals. It will, of course, involve taking the long-term view and committing resources to long-term projects. In particular, it would require a worked-out industrial strategy covering the next twenty years, of the kind which MITI produces for Japan PLC. Ours would have to be a much more developed and toughened indicative plan.

Any such strategy would have to begin from a careful consideration of potential. Perhaps the strongest potential in the region is a combination of skills (craft, technical, design and managerial) in engineering, and in particular in engineering which relates to energy projects. For example, the world's green agenda *Save Your Local Planet* will require innovations in the design and production of energy-generating devices. Of particular interest are the kind of offshore structures which will be necessary for wave power-generation. Here, the skill complex of the parent Shipbuilding and its children of Power-Generating and Offshore Production could come together. There are other potentials which need planned consideration. The region has strong historic links through the Baltic and Archangel-Murmansk with Eastern Europe and Russia. These trading connections could be revived, in association with Scandinavia and North Germany, as part of a Northern European axis which could rival the logic of development currently being drawn towards the South-East and the Channel Tunnel.

Politically, the issue is: how are people to have any chance of getting what they want when they are governed by a regime, its agencies and its collaborators, all of which are promoting a vastly different set of social objectives and economic means? The immediate answer has to be through constitutional reform. In their minority report to the 1973 *Royal Commission on the Constitution*, Crowther-Hunt and Peacock recognised that the present constitutional arrangements in the UK were inappropriate for a modern democracy. Unlike the majority of the Commission, they appreciated that this was a matter not so much of residual nationalist sentiment in Scotland and Wales as of the domination of the peripheral, industrial and, although they did not say so, working-class regions of the UK by a far-distant administrative machine derived from Tudor absolutism. They proposed a system of regional assemblies which they recognised was really the first step towards a federal state. Clearly, Crowther-Hunt and Peacock were well aware that it was likely that the federal state would not be the United Kingdom, but a United Europe composed of regions rather than existing, obsolete, nation-states.

In their 1987 pamphlet, Tyne and Wear 2000 drew up the outline of *A Regional Government for the North of England* which was modelled on the status of the (then) West German *Länder*. The idea of regional government has recently become popular with the Labour Party nationally as a way of placating Celtic nationalism, and with the Northern Labour elite. At the 1990 Regional Conference of the Labour Party, Giles Radice MP presented *A Plan for Regional Government*. Although this involved a commitment to the ultimate principle of an elected regional government, the Northern group of MPs argued for a 'step-by-step' approach which would begin with an enhancement of the existing undemocratic, corporatist, regional system by the establishment of a regional development agency and a Northern equivalent of the Scottish Office.

At least the Northern group of Labour MPs did envisage a proper regional government eventually. In a discussion paper prepared by the leader of the Durham County Council Labour group described as a *Programme for Implementation*, things were to stop for review at the intermediate corporatist stage without any directly elected assembly. Instead, there would be a '*Northern Development Council*', including 'representatives from local authorities, trades unions, the business community, northern MPs and other regional interests such as higher education institutions'. This tried, tested and failed piece of corporate nonsense is currently being hawked around Labour local government in the North-East for general endorsement.

It seems abundantly clear that only proper, democratically based, regional control over economic development and industrial policy will allow the North-East to have any chance of achieving the decent future its people so clearly want. Even then, things will not be easy. Social Democracy in one region is not possible. The region and its political institutions will have to play a part, not just in the pursuit of democratic socialist objectives in an enlarged federal Europe, which must include the former USSR and particularly the Russian Republic, but in a world in which the unequal relations between 'North' and 'South' have to be changed too. The economy which needs to be reordered is the world economy, but, to amend the pretty sensible green slogan, for the moment it is a matter of thinking globally and acting regionally.

CHAPTER THREE

Newcastle – Capital of What?

BILL LANCASTER

FIRST-TIME VISITORS TO NEWCASTLE, more often than not, experience the shattering of old illusions. Historically, England's most northern city has been viewed from afar with the outlines of the bridges barely perceptible through the smoke and grime of heavy industrial Tyneside. What lies beyond has been doubly shrouded by an equally impenetrable dialect and a culture that to outsiders appears to be both gauche and un-English. Better stay on the train or the Al until you hit the more secure terra firma of Edinburgh. At least, there, the bagpipes, Tattoo and cultured lowland drawl fit easily into the mental map of the British Isles. Tyneside also twitches a not-quite-forgotten nerve in the English psyche. Wasn't it somewhere up here that a town was murdered? All those dreadful photographs of grey, ragged men, as cold as wet clay, standing hopelessly on street corners with urchin children? 'Still closing down shipyards, I hear, and of course the coalmines ...' 'But isn't there some guy building shopping malls on top of slag heaps? ...' Better go to the 125 Buffet or wait till the next Little Chef. 'Perhaps after Edinburgh we could go to Glasgow for the day. It's been smartened up they tell me. Smashing art galleries and architecture. All the grime's gone and the working class have stopped smoking and no longer carry razors ...' Newcastle, unlike Glasgow, has yet to be socially sanitised, and its citizens have yet to have their cultural weapons confiscated. But braver travellers who alight at Central Station and head north into the city will experience one of Britain's best examples of urban sociability.

FIGURE 3.1: 'Decades before Haussmann was given his Parisian carte blanche from Louis Bonaparte, Messrs Grainger and Dobson were completing the first comprehensive rebuilding of a modern city.' *Central Station, Newcastle upon Tyne* (1850), Watercolour, John Dobson (1787–1865) and John Wilson Carmichael (1799–1868): Laing Art Gallery, Newcastle upon Tyne (Tyne and Wear Museums).

Let us first dispose of a myth. Newcastle is not an industrial city. Tyneside is, of course, a conurbation that in the recent past was dominated by heavy industry. Nineteenth-century Newcastle did have some working coalmines, but, as these became exhausted, the relentless rise of the region's 'carboniferous capitalism' took place outside the city walls. Newcastle's primary functions over the last two centuries have been commerce and consumption. A century and a half ago, the city was the equivalent of present-day Dallas. North-East grandees controlled the market of the most important commodity in the world – coal. Thanks to the control that Newcastle Corporation held over the river, the city became fat on the back of the region's muck and toil.

This richness was, and is, expressed first and foremost through the beauty and grandeur of Newcastle's architecture. Decades before Haussmann was given his Parisian carte blanche from Louis Bonaparte, Messrs Grainger and Dobson were completing the first comprehensive rebuilding of a modern city (see Figure 3.1). Despite the intervention of 1960s brutal modernism and its accompaniment of post-modernist junk bricolage, the honeystone late Georgian legacy still dominates. Moreover, Newcastle's international economic importance continued up until 1914. The glories of the Victorian infill to 'Graingertown' – Moseley Street, Neville Street, Dean Street and the far end of Grainger Street – are a constant reminder of Newcastle's nineteenth-century business confidence. Emmerson Chambers more than equals Salmon's Glaswegian 'Hatrack' in *fin-de-siècle* architectural excess, while the other great local essays of its author (pub architect Benjamin Simpson) await acknowledgement.

Much of central Newcastle was built to accommodate the business and commercial needs of the region's industrial base, but this is, and was, no 'city' of the north whose character was determined and shaped by upper-class financiers. Commerce was always rivalled and usually beaten by consumption in the battle to determine the city's character. The centrepiece of 'Graingertown' is the indoor market. This Grade 1 listed building is arguably Britain's finest, but don't expect to find twee 'festival retailing' à la Covent Garden here. Moreover, vegetarians would be well advised to give it a miss. Primarily designed as a meat market, butchery still dominates its activities, and, like most of the great Victorian indoor markets, its clientele came from all social classes. Since 1837,

Tynesiders have poured into the Grainger Market to compare and, in the early days, haggle over prices. Democracy was built into the architecture of Newcastle, and it is surely no accident that that other great example of nineteenth-century consumer democracy, the department store, was born in Newcastle when Emerson Muschamp Bainbridge established his store in a Grainger and Dobson building facing the market in the late 1830s.

So far, I have listed a series of superlatives about Newcastle's built environment. But surely many other Victorian cities experienced similar developments? This is, of course, undeniable, but Newcastle's uniqueness lies in the degree to which it has been able to retain that nineteenth-century vitality. The bleak, central urban wastelands of Liverpool, Leeds and Manchester are absent, as are the tried and failed postwar city-centre developments of Birmingham and Coventry. Instead, Newcastle contains England's second-biggest shopping centre, uniquely served by the nation's finest and most modern underground railway. Property values on Northumberland Street can exceed those of Oxford Street, while the pre-Christmas take at Marks & Spencer exceeds that of the company's Marble Arch branch. Manchester's Arndale Centre regularly suffers from thirty per cent of its units being unlet. Eldon Square has retailers queuing up for potential vacancies. What's going on? Why has contemporary Newcastle succeeded where its nineteenth-century counterparts failed? No amount of quantitative social science nor geographical accounting will answer this conundrum. Instead, Newcastle's unique commercial success is inextricably linked to its hold over the region's sense of pride in its cultural separateness.

Newcastle is much bigger than its political boundaries. Its hold over industrial Northumberland is unchallenged, and its fiefdom covers the south banks of the Tyne and down into pit-village Durham as far as that maddeningly undefined border where Sunderland loyalties take over. The city's pull also extends west through the Tyne Gap into Cumbria. Historically, Newcastle has been more accessible to Cumbrians than other major northern cities. Moreover, Cumbria's nineteenth-century burgeoning iron and coal industry often had close links with Tyneside. Cumbrian pits were often supervised by Tyneside viewers, working for owners who had interests in both areas. Newcastle has retained its economic links with its western hinterland in the twentieth century through retailing – buses from Cumbria pour daily into Eldon Square – and through the city's cultural dominance. Until the emergence of Border TV, local television for Cumbrians came from Newcastle stations, and Newcastle is still the nearest venue for major concerts and cultural events. This western connection was further strengthened by the role played by the people from the North Pennines in the development of Newcastle and Tyneside. Local coalowners favoured the God-fearing Methodists from the upper valley areas as workers, and it was two North Pennine drapers, Bainbridge and Fenwick, who established two of Newcastle's most enduring institutions.

Geography is an important factor in Newcastle's status as the regional capital, but the city's success is more than the product of location. People do not necessarily visit regional capitals just because they are there. One only has to glance at the relative decline of Liverpool and Birmingham, largely by competition from shire towns such as Chester and Leamington, to realise this point. Newcastle is, of course, surrounded by potential county rivals after the purses of the more prosperous shopper. Hexham, Morpeth and Durham City spring immediately to mind. But this centrifugal process, so detrimental to other regional capitals, has not taken place. Why?

Our first point in trying to answer this question is that Newcastle is more than just a regional capital. There is more to this city than shops, offices and courtrooms. There is more to this region than the neutral line of the geographer's map denoting urban conurbation. The region is a region more in a European sense than the somewhat blander portions of space which are allotted the term in England. This is not to deny that such a thing as a Yorkshire or Lancashire regional identity exists. But both of these counties contain too many foci to facilitate the tenacious regionalism of the Geordies. In short, Newcastle is the capital because it lacks rivals and has historically been allowed to impose its cultural imperialism upon the region. This is not to ignore the tensions that exist within the region over Newcastle's supremacy. Gateshead, just across the river, has long struggled to create an identity separate from its riverside neighbour. Writers as historically diverse as Dr Johnson and J. B. Priestley have added insult to Gateshead's sense of injury. Yet despite the town's Stadium, Garden Festival and Metro Centre, it remains, in essence, a suburb of Newcastle. Nothing illustrates this point more than a walk along any of the bridges across the Tyne in either the morning or evening rush hour. In Gateshead, 'all roads lead to Newcastle'. Sunderland has long offered a more tenacious resistance to the hegemony of Newcastle. Possessing its own football team and brewery has assisted this resistance, while its now lost industry of shipbuilding provided another source of rivalry. Yet the recent collapse of shipbuilding and the controversy that surrounded its demise were perceived as a regional injury – yet another kick in the teeth from London, injuries that go back to Jarrow and beyond. In the same vein, Nissan cars are referred to and perceived to be a regional product as much as a Sunderland one. Sunderland awaits connection to the Metro system, and the ambivalence of many of its local politicians to such a link illustrates the fragility of its sense of separateness from Newcastle.

Geography and history have undoubtedly given the city many advantages in its hold over the region, but what needs to be explained is how Newcastle has retained and increased its dominance. Again, we must return to the wider regional experience for part of our answer. The long depression of the interwar period was accompanied by the growth of new national media forms. The radio and the cinema articulated images and definitions of British, and more often English, life that rarely gave space to the Geordie experience. Even the emergence of regional television in the postwar period gave scant regard to local culture in its early years. This writer can still remember being bussed into the City Road Studios in the early 1960s to be part of the audience for the station's window on local life, *The One O'Clock Show* – hardly a prime-time programme. The film *Payroll* of the same period was filmed in and based upon Newcastle. We flocked to see it. The leading actors had refined southern accents, the actresses behaved and talked like debutantes, while the locals were kept at a safe distance. Indeed, when they were allowed to talk, such as in the riverside pub scene, cockney accents were used! This process of being isolated from the larger national culture served to intensify a sense of regional identity. The 1950s and 1960s saw the rise of Bobby Thompson, a comedian with phenomenal local success, whose humour could never travel further south than Billingham. The number of leek shows grew, an avalanche of Geordie kitsch books and pamphlets was produced, and even our previously unremarked-upon bread,

Stotty Cake, developed a 'Stottyrama' bakery in the Grainger Market. Sport, particularly football, served a similar cultural purpose.

It would, however, be a mistake to exaggerate this process of marginalisation. The Geordies did not become cultural Luddites. One response of being overlooked by national culture was to celebrate what was physically disappearing. Another was to blend a growing sense of regional identity with an active participation in national life. Local pop stars from The Animals via Sting to the Pet Shop Boys have proved particularly adept at artistic creativity at a national level. Retaining a sense of the past does not necessarily involve a rejection of the modern. Contemporary Newcastle's acknowledged vitality owes much to this combination of past and present.

CARNIVAL

The two decades after the Second World War may have witnessed the region's continuing cultural isolation, but the region did share in the nation's rising prosperity. To be sure, the region did lag behind the nation on all economic indicators, but cheaper housing and transport costs took some of the edge off this differential. More money meant more consumption, and the Geordies reverted to their nineteenth-century noisy confidence. The 'Bonny Toon' with its 'characters', heavy drinking and good-natured sociability was central to the popular culture that emerged in the nineteenth century. The Bigg Market was as noisy in the 1890s as it is in the 1990s. The local nineteenth-century temperance campaigners knew what they were doing when they erected the Bigg Market drinking fountain with the inscription 'Water is Best'. Unfortunately for them, there is little evidence of their advice being heeded in that quarter. Paradoxically, the failure of the nineteenth-century advocates of 'rational recreation' has given rise to the city's two most important modern characteristics: a carnivalesque atmosphere and a strong sense of classlessness.

The idea of 'carnival' is currently much in vogue with cultural theorists in their search for deeper meanings in past literature. The notion, however, can also be fruitfully used in probing Newcastle's vibrant popular culture. The best carnivals usually occur in marketplaces, and this is certainly the case in Newcastle (see Figure 3.2). Moreover, the celebration is a daily rather than an intermittent event. Note how the character and the ethos of the central area undergo rapid daily changes. During the day, the streets are generally bustling with shoppers and appear similar to, if busier than, many other city centres. The Bigg Market, with its entrance to a department store, newspaper offices, street fruit market, specialist shops, fast-food outlets and half-empty bars, during the day functions like any other commercial thoroughfare. Yet, in the early evening, its character undergoes a dramatic renegotiation. Five o'clock sees the start of 'Happy Hour' in the bars and the arrival of the first wave of revellers. The rules of the street are radically changed. The pensive shopper is replaced by the garrulous celebrant. The first waves of revellers are often women escaping from the monotony of the office and shop counter. The decorous behaviour of the workplace is soon replaced by noisy talk. Outside, the streets rapidly fill as crowds pour in from all parts of the conurbation and beyond. Visitors from outside the region are

FIGURE 3.2: 'The best carnivals usually occur in marketplaces, and this is certainly the case in Newcastle.' *Newcastle's Bigg Market* (1988), Photograph: Newcastle upon Tyne Libraries and Arts.

often staggered by the scale of the event. There is nothing like the Bigg Market anywhere else in Britain; only the Reeperbahn in Hamburg stands comparison.

The evening carnival of central Newcastle witnesses other changes and social redefinitions. Carnivals are popular celebrations combined with both audacious and subtle challenges to conventional life and modes of behaviour. The dress of the participants is louder and noticeably different from that worn by revellers elsewhere in Britain. Outsiders are first struck by the number of women. The Bigg Market is not a male drinking binge. Women are there in equal numbers. Many dress to shock – scanty mini-dresses in the midst of winter are not unusual. But there is nothing debauched or sexist in this phenomenon. Indeed, the Bigg Market is a curiously feminist experience. The women equal the men in behaviour as well as numbers. Provocatively dressed, they play the men at their own macho game in this curious deconstruction of courtship and social conventions.

The men, on the other hand, are performing a social ritual, the origins of which can be traced back to the early nineteenth century and beyond. The 'Bonny Pit Laddie' was always a flashy dresser. His display of bright colour was usually allied with an aura of 'hardness' (see Figure 3.3). 'Bigg Marketeers' rarely wear coats or jackets. T-shirts or short-sleeved shirts are the norm, with no regard to season; 'hard Geordie lads' are not supposed to feel the cold.

By nine o'clock, when the carnival is in full swing, we can witness the true paradox of late-twentieth-century Newcastle sociability. 'Pit-hardened' young males, with no pit or shipyard within which to vent their machismo, sublimate their traditional industrial toughness into the carnivalesque. Work is now provided in offices, shops, light industry or an employment scheme, but these males are even more aware of their birthright of a 'good neet in the toon' than their fathers were. As in so many other areas of North-East society, regional culture has survived industrial disintegration. Indeed, it could be argued that the carnivalisation of popular culture provides a vital emotional prop for coping with rapid change. For women, however, the Bigg Market has a different meaning. Their participation signifies their emancipation, and what better place to show it than in that most prized male institution – the pub?

FIGURE 3.3: 'The "Bonny Pot Laddie" was always a flashy dresser. His display of bright colour was usually allied with an aura of "Lardness".' *Two young men* (1958), Photograph: courtesy of Jimmy Forsyth and West Newcastle Local Studies Centre (from *Scotswood Road*, Bloodaxe Books, 1986).

The Bigg Market rarely erupts into violence. The police have an expert understanding of the event and even refer to the Bigg Market beat as community policing. Their manner and style changes from the daytime norm to that of a friendly big brother keeping an eye on the youngsters' party. The Bigg Market is in many ways a successful representation of a virulent regional culture coping with social change. But there is also a downside to local male machismo. Participation in the carnival requires clothes (often expensive), money to spend and the taxi fare home. Moreover, participation signifies membership of a wider culture of consumption: football matches, videos and foreign holidays are all part of the same currency. For those with little or no access to this lifestyle, 'hardness' is often translated into something much sourer. Six cars every day end up as burned wrecks, while many more are stolen. It is far too simple to equate money with the Bigg Market and lack of it with ram-raiding. But as Paul Willis has clearly shown in his writing, young working-class machismo served the function of socialising youngsters into the life of heavy or monotonous manual labour. Yet, in places like Elswick and Meadow Well, industrial work is becoming a folk memory, something that Grandad did. Many families are now entering a third decade of giro-dependency, while the almost sacred sites of work on the riverbank are being transformed into marina villages and information technology offices. This produces more than a few cruel geographical juxtapositions. Walker looks down to the high-class housing and private yachts of St Peter's basin; Elswick and Benwell have visually witnessed the bulldozing of Armstrong's and the building of the Business Park; North Shields sees the decline of an industrial waterfront being replaced by upmarket housing. It is no surprise that this disintegration of the old landscape and of the economic and social order which it supported is accompanied by social trauma.

Despite claims to the contrary from Conservative politicians, Geordies did riot in the 1930s. The disturbances in North Shields in November 1932 were more than the equal of recent disorder, while earlier in that year a demonstration of 100,000 people on the Town Moor posed a serious threat to Newcastle. But there are major differences between recent events and the 1930s. Anger and frustration in the earlier period had a political focus and gave rise to organisation and marches by the unemployed. This is understandable, as the solution to unemployment was visible to all who had eyes to see. Pits and shipyards were idle, yet pregnant with the solution to social distress. Jarrow was murdered, but this only knocked one hole in the Tyne's industrial wall. Today, little is left of this industrial riverscape. All that is being offered to fill the void is an ill-fitting facade of 1980's architectural fantasy.

This phenomenon is not unique to Newcastle and Tyneside. Many conurbations in the last few decades have produced geographical and social wastelands and witnessed the growth of communities that are virtually dependent on welfare. Tyneside, however, is an old industrial area, with perhaps the oldest working-class culture. Local inhabitants have a remarkable talent for cultural transformation, providing they can participate in the new. The denial of this option witnesses another transformation into anger, despair and the most distressing forms of communal self-mutilation.

Newcastle has other unique cultural practices which are as important as popular consumption. Away from the noisy environs of the Bigg Market, the carnival goes on. The city has six theatres including the Theatre Royal, the RSC's third home. Yet the most interesting productions tend to take place in the smaller auditoriums. One of the most enjoyable venues is the Live Theatre on the Quayside. Here, the typical format is the audience seated around small tables, with drinks from the bar, watching productions by the region's burgeoning group of playwrights. This is Geordie high culture, but a world away from the velvet plush and the dulcet tones of conventional theatre. The 'Live's' most successful productions are usually local in content and rich in dialect. Moreover, the audience often defies generalisation in terms of age and class. They come to see plays about Jack Common, North Shields fisherfolk and Bigg Market nights out which are invariably of a high dramatic standard and which at the same time celebrate, probe and affirm the power of regional cultural identity.

A night at the 'Live' offers the essence of Newcastle. The walk along the Quay below the soaring bridges then up Dean Street and Grey Street passes buildings which at night can appear almost magical. In the space of a few hours, it is possible to experience art, culture, magnificent architecture and good food, but the paradox of this urban treat is that the poison of class pretentiousness that pervades a 'cultural' night in most cities is virtually non-existent.

In a curious sense, Newcastle is a classless city. How can such a statement about a gritty northern city be justified?

CLASS

Social anthropologists have often pointed out that to end the caste system in India it is necessary to eradicate the Brahmin, not 'untouchability'. This is precisely what has happened in Newcastle. The city's value system, politics, myths and symbols are essentially working-class. This is not to deny the existence of a local middle class, nor indeed that of an elite. A walk through gentrified Jesmond, past the Real Tennis court into well-manicured Gosforth, or a journey to 'Little Chigwell' at Darras Hall makes it abundantly clear that the city does not lack a well-heeled middle class. Moreover, like middle-class suburbs in other cities, they have their cordons sanitaires to ensure spatial separation from the lower orders. Jesmond has the canyon of the Dean to define clearly its border with working-class Heaton; Gosforth sits beyond the Town Moor; while the suburban enclave of Darras Hall is over the fields and far away. The city also possesses an unusually high number of private schools and elite institutions such as the Literary and Philosophical Society, the Natural History Society and the Northern Counties Club. Recent events have also shown that old money still dominates the affairs of Newcastle United, and old families such as the Cooksons, Ridleys and Strakers still exert local influence. Despite this considerable presence, the local rich have not been able to establish a cultural hegemony over the city and its region. Indeed, if we poke and probe the thicket of middle-class Newcastle, we are struck by the degree of cultural identity that it shares with the working class.

Explore this point by starting at the Collingwood Arms in Brandling Village. This pub is the local of middle-class Jesmond and the former pupils of the Royal Grammar School. Frequented by business people, professionals and the youth of the Newcastle rich, this pub can be as noisy and raucous as any in the Bigg Market. Jesmond, however, was not always like this. In the second decade of the twentieth century, the suburb was the subject of a cruel but humorous novel by the Russian Yevgeny Zamyatin. In his work, *Islanders*, he depicts a community of sombre, liquorice-dressed men and women terrified of breaking social conventions and existing in a world isolated from the grimmer and noisier realities of working-class life. According to Zamyatin, the Jesmondites excelled themselves on Sunday:

> By Sunday the stone steps of the houses in Jesmond had as usual been scrubbed to a dazzling whiteness. The houses were old and smoke-blackened but the steps shone in white rows, like the Sunday gentlemen's false teeth. The Sunday gentlemen were, of course, manufactured at a factory in Jesmond, and on a Sunday morning thousands of copies appeared on the streets, ... carrying identical canes and wearing identical top hats, the respectable Sunday gentlemen in their false teeth strolled down the street and greeted their doubles.

In the 1920s, the novelist Rosamund Lehman, in her *A Note in Music*, gave a similar depiction.

Jesmond today is a world away from the stuffy conformity that characterised the suburb in the first half of this century. The Geordie youngish middle class pose as they shop in Acorn Road; their accent may not be as broad as elsewhere in the city, but there are few attempts to disguise it. Moreover, the exclusivity of Jesmond is breaking down. People from less salubrious suburbs feel at home in the pubs, wine bars and restaurants of Newcastle's Mayfair. This is a far cry from the experience of young Jack Common, whose first visit to Jesmond early this century was recorded in *Kiddar's Luck* with the sense of discovery usually reserved for Victorian explorers. If the region's greatest and funniest writer found Jesmond alien and un-Geordie, it is a measure of the erosion of cultural class barriers that *Viz*, the quintessential expression of local irreverence to English conformity, is largely the product of Jesmond middle-class youth.

This dominance of regional over class identity is expressed in many facets of everyday Newcastle. The city's middle class vote Labour in increasing numbers, and Conservatism has but a scant presence on the local council. This is not because the middle class are becoming socialist, but because for a wide range of reasons they perceive Labour as best expressing the region's interests. Further, the cultural convergence of class has resulted in other social groups being more sympathetic to working-class needs and interests. Thatcherism always found Newcastle barren soil. This is no great surprise. The local middle class consists of an unusually high percentage of public-sector workers. Even the growth of the private-sector middle class is often rooted in indigenous working-class origins. Thus, unemployment in the 1980s was often experienced by middle-class families – if not directly, almost certainly by their relatives. Mrs Thatcher's claim that society doesn't exist is a nonsense in Newcastle. It is impossible to dodge the poor when they are family, friends and those you went to school with. In an area where a large proportion of families are only a generation removed from mining and heavy industry, older solidarities still matter, and paradoxically the Thatcher decade has served to bind the community closer together.

These cultural and political themes are reinforced by the city's, and indeed the region's, historical self-image. The most notable local museums, Beamish, The Science and Military Vehicle collections and numerous industrial heritage sites display a strong, deep-rooted pride in the region's industrial past. The city does possess an art gallery, the Laing, which contains works of national importance, but significantly the gallery's biggest crowd-puller for many years was the recent Ralph Hedley exhibition. Hedley's paintings of romanticised pit scenes and working-class street life may not be great art, but their contribution to contemporary self-identity remains profound. Armstrong's, Parson's and Swan Hunter's are still powerful totems in the collective Geordie psyche. It is a past that, along with coalmining, is rapidly vanishing, and some writers even talk of a post-industrial Tyneside. This fervour for industrial heritage transcends class. This is a very different situation from that which currently prevails in Glasgow. In that city, which shares a very similar history to Newcastle, a sustained programme of cultural redefinition has been under way for a number of years. The perpetrators of this exercise have been highly successful in rewriting Glasgow's history. One and a half centuries of heavy industrialisation rarely account for more than a few sentences in the city guides and tourist brochures. Instead, Glasgow chooses to give pride of place to the artistic good taste of a handful of Victorian capitalists. Glaswegians are being advised to forget their long history of iron, steel, heavy engineering and shipbuilding and instead give prominence to a few art collections, artists and architects, all of whom had previously only existed at the margins of the city's life. On a recent visit, the present writer found the menu in a transport cafe written in Mackintosh lettering! Glasgow's artistic heritage does deserve the praise that it is currently receiving. But one wonders how ordinary Glaswegians feel at this covering-up of the experiences and history of generations of their forebears. Outsiders may find the Geordie obsession with industrial history to be an indicator of the region's backwardness, while theorists may criticise the heritage industry as invented kitsch, but both miss the significance of how historical experience, mythology and legends can strengthen communities and serve to overcome internal antagonisms. Bill Williamson explores this theme more fully in Chapter 9.

This sense of community and a common culture can also have economic benefits. The region is undoubtedly no longer the heavy industrial powerhouse of earlier decades, but a walk around central Newcastle does not give the impression of economic decline. Instead, the image of consumer prosperity dominates. Recent writers on Britain's retail industry have tried to account for Newcastle's stunning shopping boom. Lower living costs and higher-than-average ratios of disposable income, together with Britain's best public transport system, all play a part in the city's success. But these factors do not explain the whole story. Some commentators have noted the similarities between Oxford Street and the Northumberland Street/Eldon Square complex in terms of property prices and store turnover. This point is nearer the mark. Oxford Street is successful because everyone can go there without fear of having their status sensibilities affronted. Northumberland Street gives off similar vibrations, but for very different reasons. To understand its success, we need to examine the street's history.

Northumberland Street as a shopping venue was invented by J.J. Fenwick when he opened an upmarket gown and draper's shop in what was then a fashionable residential street occupied by professionals and the Northumbrian gentry. His skill as a fashion designer soon won him a clientele from the gentry, aristocracy and national personalities such as Dame Ellen Terry. Crowds from all social classes flocked to view the windows of the city's finest carriage trade store, and other retailers soon moved into nearby properties to capitalise on the growth of pavement traffic. The real revolution of Northumberland Street, however, occurred in the 1890s when J. J. Fenwick's two sons, Fred and Arthur, returned from Paris, where their father had sent them to study the fashion trade. Fred in particular was deeply impressed by the success of the

Bon Marché department store. This *grand magasin* had pioneered the concept of the 'democratisation of luxury', which allowed anyone to enter, wander around and examine clearly priced goods. It also developed the sense of spectacle and theatre which tantalised shoppers – ideas borrowed from the Parisian great exhibitions. Against their father's wishes, the brothers changed the Northumberland Street store's merchandising policies, and its enlarged facade was designed in a similar style to the Bon Marché. This was a social revolution of immense importance. A pitman's wife could now shop in the same store as the Duchess of Northumberland. Fenwick's continued to cater for the top end of the market while sucking in the ordinary shoppers by their thousands. The store managed to combine the class of Harrods with the classlessness of Selfridge's without the geographical separation of Oxford Street and Knightsbridge. Moreover, this was achieved almost ten years before Selfridge embarked on his Oxford Street venture.

Fenwick's continues to present a similar democratic image. The aristocracy may not be so apparent in the Northumberland Street store, but there is continuity in the store's merchandising that crosses many class barriers. Start in the basement where the paint is as cheap as in the out-of-town DIY sheds, go upstairs through the clothes where the price and quality gradually rise, up to the chandeliered French Salon where everything seems to cost three figures and the clientele is very Darras Hall. Or, better still, the Delicatessen, where bags of crisps battle for shelf space with foreign exotica. There is none of Harrods Food Hall's sustained snobbishness here! The democratic aspect of Fenwick's has, of course, been a well-nurtured policy for virtually a century. Consider the Blackett Street entrance. It is the store's window on the west, whose art deco facade, built in the late 1930s, is designed to draw in the less prosperous shoppers from the west end who had traditionally confined themselves to Clayton Street and the Grainger Market. To return to an earlier point, Oxford Street succeeds because of anonymity, while Northumberland Street/Eldon Square equals London's major shopping venue because Geordie shoppers have a deep cultural awareness of the 'democracy of luxury'. Newcastle owes much to Fenwick's, perhaps the region's most successful business.

Cultural and social theorists have often derided the rise of consumer society. Many see it as eroding older, more meaningful solidarities. The faceless shopping mall, with its empty promise of purchasing satisfaction, is often contrasted with close-knit local communities, pubs, clubs and Saturday afternoon football matches. The workers, they argue, have traded their sense of class for a pocketful of plastic. There may be something in this observation, but it may also reflect the prejudices of an elite. Observers of shoppers in Newcastle will gain a different impression. On any Saturday, the crowds appear overwhelming. Geordies have been famous for conspicuous consumption for centuries. The city has more flower shops per head than any other city. Yet, because they have been doing it so long, they have become good at it. The clothes, to outsiders, often seem loud and gaudy, but it must be kept in mind that the Geordie dresses for Geordie eyes. Geordie youth has always been showy and noisy, and postwar demographic trends have, in recent years, given the city an unusually high proportion of youngsters. Their presence is inescapable; but look closer, notice the number of tattoos and unashamedly displayed love-bites – such marks can offend outsiders. Conversations are noisy rantings, and each voice seems to compete for dialectal distinctiveness. Older people seem unperturbed by such boisterousness – 'Just bairns having a bit daft carry-on' is the usual response. It is here, amid the beautiful buildings of 'Graingertown', the flower stalls, brash clothes, loud talk, well-patronised buskers, the liveliest pubs in England and a population that so often appears to break the rules of national reserve – by being incredibly friendly and irreverent – that we come to the heart of Newcastle.

CHAPTER FOUR

The Drama of the North-East

ALAN PLATER

IT IS A UNIVERSAL TRUTH that we have no control over our place of birth, but we live with the consequences for ever. Jack Common, in his bobby-dazzling opening chapter of *Kiddar's Luck*, entitled 'Blunder By An Unborn Babe', analyses the dilemma thus:

> There were plenty of golden opportunities going that night. In palace and mansion flat, in hall and manor and new central-heated 'cottage', the wealthy, talented and beautiful lay coupled – welcome wombs were ten-a-penny, must have been. What do you think I picked on, me and my genes, that is? Missing lush Sussex, the Surrey soft spots, affluent Mayfair and gold-filled Golders Green, fat Norfolk rectories, the Dukeries, and many a solid Yorkshire village, to name only some obvious marks, I came upon the frost-rimed roofs of a working-class suburb in Newcastle-upon-Tyne [see Figure 4.1], and in the back-bedroom of an upstairs flat in a street parallel with the railway line, on which a halted engine whistled to be let through the junction, I chose my future parents. There, it was done. By the time that engine took its rightaway and rolled into the blue glare of the junction arcs, another kiddar was started, an event, one might add, of no novelty in that quarter and momentous only to me.

I was born in Jarrow in 1935, and my father, like Will Kiddar's, (and, for the record, Jack Common's) worked on the railway. There the resemblance ends, and my timing was much better. Common grew up as a writer when the proletarian novelist, whether from the North-East or South Wales or Clydeside, was worth a casual aside over dinner in Bloomsbury, but was unlikely

FIGURE 4.1: 'Missing lush Sussex, the Surrey soft spots, affluent Mayfair and
gold-filled Golders Green, fat Norfolk rectories, the Dukeries, and many a solid
Yorkshire village, ... I came upon the frost-rimed roofs of a working-class suburb
in Newcastle-upon-Tyne ... ' *Pitboys at Boldon Colliery* – 'Wheel Them In' (1921),
Photograph: South Tyneside Libraries.

to be offered a seat at the table and a square meal. I grew up as a
writer in the 1960s, when the rapid expansion of television created a
more congenial marketplace for non-metropolitan dramatists.
Since most of the viewers were non-metropolitan – certainly in the
Bloomsbury sense – they were happy to share our stories. *Coronation
Street* and *Z Cars* were early proof. It was a simple, mathematical
equation. We could deliver audiences; therefore we got the job.

I wrote eighteen scripts for *Z Cars* during the years 1963-5. The
setting was 'Newtown', a fictional version of Kirkby, which is, in
real life, a satellite town of Liverpool, close to Aintree racecourse
and, at that time, part of Harold Wilson's parliamentary constitu-
ency. The series was garlanded with praise and awards, and the
critical consensus said: this is a definitive picture of the area. Gritty
realism ruled, and it was OK. But scratch any critical consensus
and it will bleed contradictions and paradoxes.

The original streetwise coppers in *Z Cars* were played by Jimmy

Ellis from Ireland, Joe Brady from Scotland and the Yorkshiremen, Brian Blessed and Jeremy Kemp. Their immediate superior, Sergeant Watt, was played by Frank Windsor from the Midlands, and his superior, Inspector Barlow, by Stratford Johns, who was born in South Africa.

A similar pattern applied to the writers. None of the regular team came from Liverpool, and I was the only one who lived outside of London. My family had moved to Hull in 1938, where I stayed until 1984, apart from university days in Newcastle during the 1950s. Hull is very different from Liverpool. Ask anyone in Hull or Liverpool. Of the other writers, John Hopkins and Troy Kennedy Martin were enormously talented south-country chaps, Keith Dewhurst was from Manchester and Allan Prior was a Geordie who had found his way to St Albans by way of Blackpool.

To be sure, Liverpool was a racial melting pot but, in retrospect, a vital ingredient seems to have been missing from *Z Cars*. We had to wait for Neville Smith, Alan Bleasdale and Willy Russell for the bred-in-the-bone insider's vision of the city.

The show reflected the overall picture in film and television drama of the early 1960s. The non-metropolitan piece became a genre in its own right. At the crassest level, it was good box office. But the setting was an ill-defined, generalised lump of the good earth called 'The North', and the writers were categorised as 'Northern writers'. Hull-born Tom Courtenay starred in *Billy Liar*, despite its West Riding setting, and Salford-born Albert Finney found his way to Nottingham in *Saturday Night and Sunday Morning*, all without comment in the posh newspapers, though there were comments aplenty in the areas listed. But near enough was, generally speaking, near enough.

I cannot tell a lie. I played the game happily along with everyone else, in radio, theatre and television. Bliss it was to be working in an industry which required up to three hundred original television plays per annum, and I even invented a geographical area for the purpose, enshrined in the stage direction:

'The play is set in an industrial town somewhere in the Mid-Pennines.'

This gave us a licence to cast any actor within a radius of a hundred miles of Bradford or Wakefield. In practice, we went even further afield. My heroes of the time tended to be young, sensitive and

FIGURE 4.2: 'Drama schools taught their students to speak "properly" – a quaint form of English located halfway between Broadcasting House and Buckingham Palace . . . ' *Listening to the Wireless* (1930s), Photograph: South Tyneside Libraries.

misunderstood (for some reason I cannot fathom), and they were played at various times by London-born Alfred Lynch and Welsh-born Hywel Bennet. I took Hywel to the dog-track in Hull so he could study the neighbourhood vowel sounds. Both he and Alfie played the heartbeat of their characters to perfection; but they both had trouble with the short 'a', as in 'having a bath' or 'going to the dance'.

There was an institutionalised problem within the acting profession. Drama schools taught their students to speak 'properly' – a quaint form of English located halfway between Broadcasting House and Buckingham Palace (see Figure 4.2) – and, if there was time to spare between sword-fencing lessons, they might throw in supplementary guidance on basic 'accents' – sufficient to stumble through weekly rep productions of Walter Greenwood, Harold Brighouse and J. B. Priestley.

The obvious question on the agenda is: where was Tyneside in the midst of all this? The answer is: nowhere in particular. It was a largely unexplored patch within the larger landscape of the fictional 'North', and any actor from the region knew that his professional future depended on shedding the accent with the speed of light, or faster if possible.

In or around 1967, I wrote an episode of *Softly Softly*, a legitimate offspring of *Z Cars*, set notionally around Bristol. For reasons of plot, we needed a visiting police officer from the 'North', and the part was played by John Woodvine. I knew John's reputation as one of the finest classical actors of our time, and it came as a surprise in rehearsals when he said: 'Shall I play him as a Geordie?'

'Are you a Geordie? Where are you from?' I asked.

'I was born in Tyne Dock,' he said.

'Whyebuggaman!' I said.

The incident has considerable historical significance, for me if not for the rest of the civilised world. John was the first actor I had met who *owned up* to being from Tyneside. It was, as it turned out, a timely meeting.

A year later, in collaboration with Alex Glasgow and Sid Chaplin, I wrote *Close the Coalhouse Door* for the then Newcastle Playhouse in Jesmond. Suddenly we had to find not one actor, but an entire company capable of handling the accent. We knew about John Woodvine, but what about the others? It was time for the acting profession to own up. The director, Bill Hays, born in Wingate, County Durham, dug deeply and successfully. The most obvious 'cheat' was Staffordshire-born Bryan Pringle, who qualified on the basis that he had a wife from South Shields and an Auntie Bella in Gateshead, and was a terrific actor.

And yet we still cheated. The precise geographical setting of the show is the South-West Durham coalfield, and the only actor in the cast from that area was Kevin Stoney. In strict, though maybe pedantic terms, we were still compromising: a short step from a generalised, fictional 'North' to a generalised, fictional 'North-East'. Perhaps that is as far as we can hope to travel in the direction of the specific. If you write a play about the street where you were born and bred, you are unlikely to find a complete company of talented actors who were also born in that street. This may sound like nit-picking of cosmic proportions, but it is a real issue. I claim an ability to place any Northern accent to the nearest ten miles or so. Sid Chaplin could place people to specific areas of Newcastle by the sound of the voice.

Close the Coalhouse Door was seen on BBC Television in 1969, and, without overstating the case, it must have been one of the first networked plays written and played in full-blooded North-East accents. What followed was not exactly a deluge, but the waters of the Tyne certainly flowed with increasing vigour through the 1970s. My own contribution was to adapt A. J. Cronin's *The Stars Look Down*, seen on Granada Television in 1975. It was followed by the BBC's *When The Boat Comes In* in 1976. Both series had large casts, and Geordie actors shot out of their closets ten at a time. The really smart ones managed to be in both series and play bit parts in *The Likely Lads* as well.

The evolution of a recognisable North-East drama began in the only way possible: with the writers, on the blank sheet of paper. They are, to be sure, a diverse and unpredictable bunch. It is dangerous to play the category game, but there are three that suggest themselves: first, the native writers who stay in the area – Tom Hadaway, Leonard Barras and the late Sid Chaplin. Second, the wanderers who pitch camp somewhere else and find it impossible to leave – Phil Woods, who wrote a lovely stage version of *Kiddar's Luck*, and, of course, the great Cecil Taylor. Third, those who leave, often very early in life, but continue to be haunted by Tyneside – myself, Peter Terson, Ian La Frenais. Indeed, I always imagine Ian sitting by a swimming pool in Los Angeles, trying to get the football results on the BBC World Service.

It was the Tyneside-based writers, Tom Hadaway, Sid Chaplin and Alex Glasgow, who gave the real impetus to the memorable first series of *When The Boat Comes In*. Their work had a directness, a passion and a grace rare in the history of television series drama. Above all, their work had individuality. Each of them left unmistakable fingerprints: the authorial voice, as it is called in publishers' offices.

This may seem a crudely self-evident comment, but it flies in the face of current front-office wisdom, where television drama is processed and packaged for easy consumption, under the influence of the market forces. On a writers' panel at the Banff Television Festival in Canada in 1989, an American writer-producer called Georgia Jeffreys explained that every episode of *Cagney and Lacey* had three elements: a police story, an emotional story and a comic runner or subplot. I protested, roughly in the following terms:

'Supposing I came to you with a wonderful story that was a police story and also emotional and also comic, would I be allowed to do it?'
'No.'

'But the audience might like the series even more if you took them by surprise occasionally and let the writer's fingerprints show.'

'Sorry, Alan. The network wouldn't allow it.'

As Leonard Barras once pointed out, everything that happens in America eventually arrives here – it's something to do with the Gulf Stream. This is an elaborate way of saying that the industry has changed and that *When The Boat Comes In* could no longer happen with the same degree of creative freedom. We need to build a tidal barrier against this particular Gulf Stream – and quickly, while there's still time.

The mathematics of the situation are simple. The television industry which required three hundred original plays per annum in the 1960s can now manage with one tenth of that number, and to judge by the way they are concealed in the programme schedules, frequently finds them an embarrassment. The conditions that made possible, for example, Tom Hadaway's *God Bless Thee, Jacky Maddison*, no longer apply. The message to television writers is: write whatever you like, provided that you (a) service a long-running soap opera or (b) dramatise a quasi-classic novel or best seller or (c) have a detective or villain as your central character. The response of many writers, and as a group they are not without native cunning and a survival instinct, is to run away and hide in the nearest genre.

Dennis Potter's *The Singing Detective* and Troy Kennedy Martin's *Edge Of Darkness* were both highly individual personal statements of the kind that distinguished the single play during television drama's golden age; but they made these statements within the form of an investigative serial. I played the same game, with great joy, in the three *Beiderbecke* series, which purported to be investigative thrillers, but were also an excuse to have fun in the adventure playground at the back of my head – which is, of course, the place all the 'proper' plays come from. All these examples were, I believe, single plays dressed up as series. They also, to borrow a piece of current jargon, deconstructed their genres with more skill and less fuss than *Twin Peaks*. The slogan we used to describe Jill and Trevor, the detective duo at the centre of the *Beiderbecke* sagas, was:

'They were not brave; they were not beautiful; but they were available.'

If that's not deconstruction, I don't know what is.

In the context of the North-East, nobody has played the genre game as consistently and skilfully as Ian La Frenais. The canon, for our purposes, begins with *The Likely Lads*, played by James Bolam, born in Sunderland, and Rodney Bewes, born in Bingley in Yorkshire. Memory says it was set in the same generalised 'North' mentioned earlier, though laced with the odd Whitley Bay joke of the kind none of us can resist – and no reason to do so. In the 'easy shot' department, Whitley Bay is the North-East equivalent of Wigan and Scunthorpe.

In the early 1980s, *Auf Wiedersehen Pet* arrived on our screens. It told the stories of a gang of building workers, forced by unemployment at home into seeking honest toil in Germany. Generically it belonged to the same tradition as the *Odyssey* and the *Famous Five*; a bunch of kids having adventures. Politically it belonged to the same tradition as *Close The Coalhouse Door* and *When The Boat Comes In* – where love of the birthplace is soured by unemployment and Whitehall cynicism. The three Geordies at the heart of the gang, played by Tim Healy, Kevin Whateley and Jimmy Nail, are haunted by the North-East, especially when marooned in Germany. The theme of Geordies as a wandering tribe, looking for work and perhaps a little dignity, remains underexplored. As the son of such a wanderer, I plead guilty to this neglect.

The three actors mentioned have since become leading players in their own right, to the extent that, in 1991, Jimmy Nail starred in *Spender*, co-created with Ian La Frenais. Spender is a policeman, a Geordie living in voluntary exile in London, who is sent north to work undercover on Tyneside. The genre is, again, the investigative thriller. It is given distinction by the use of Tyneside locations, almost exclusively regional accents and a lovely cast of supporting players, with throwaway grace notes in pubs and on street corners, reminiscent of the bellhops and janitors in Philip Marlow's Los Angeles.

All this is a remarkable transformation. In the 1960s, the idea of a popular, mainstream television series, with a Geordie central character and a Tyneside setting, would have been unthinkable. Television drama was, for the most part, studio-based, which inevitably influenced the thinking of writers and producers alike. Then, the drama was enacted in a series of rooms where people talked, whether in *Hancock* or the memorable John Hopkins quartet, *Talking To A Stranger*. Location filming was a rare and expensive treat. Gradually, through the 1970s, the use of location film and video became more acceptable and now it is the bread-and-butter technology of the industry. In simple economic terms, it is usually cheaper to hire a 'real' room than to build one in a studio. But transcending technology and economics is an apparent cultural transformation. We are, as an audience, much more eager to celebrate our differences than programme controllers realise.

Twenty-five years ago, television drama was set either in a generalised Home Counties or a generalised North Country. The achievement of the writers was to smash the generalisations. Alan Bleasdale and Willy Russell defined Liverpool; John Byrne and Peter McDougall defined Glasgow; the already-mentioned tribe of writers, wanderers and otherwise defined the North-East; and all these works found a willing audience. The only surprise is that front-office executives should be surprised. *Coronation Street* found a massive, nationwide audience more or less from Episode One, as did *EastEnders* and, to move the debate on to a global scale, *Neighbours*.

Clearly, there are several contradictions lurking within the story so far. I have reported a golden age, now gone, when the single play was revered and the playwright, briefly, sat at the tables of the mighty. But I am also reporting that the viewers are more willing than ever to confront the difficult and the unfamiliar. Conclusion: the audience is being short-changed.

I was once asked by an interviewer what a writer needs more than anything else. My answer was: the shortest distance to the audience. That is a central problem facing the television writer in the 1990s. The global village is at hand, and there are more producers making deals than there are making programmes: an excellent situation for the airline industry, but not so healthy for the writers. During those youthful and innocent days on *Z Cars*, I would deliver a script and it was on the air, live, six weeks later. Now it takes six weeks to organise a Lunch, to discuss the possibility of a co-production Deal with the Americans which might lead to the writing of a Treatment, which might, after a few more lunches, lead to the writing of a Screenplay, which, after even more lunches, might turn into a Television Movie. Do not mistake this for exaggeration.

The heart of the matter, as ever and always, is the control of production and distribution. Our colleagues in the American

Writers' Guild commissioned a report on the future of the mass media, and the prediction was that, by the turn of the century, world television could be controlled by four men – presumably with names like Murdoch and Berlusconi. Making due allowance for the fact that economists making predictions have a track record on a par with entrail-readers, it is nonetheless an alarming proposition.

There are obvious parallels with the feature-film industry. The Americans saw, long ago, that the secret of success was to control the means of distribution and exhibition. Once that was established, the problem of *what* to distribute and exhibit was almost incidental. The logical conclusion of this system is a film called *Ninja Enforcer's Godfather Three*.

The problem for the British is that we share a language with the Americans, but a culture with Europe. Our creative writers and programme-makers are, by nature, subversive. Those who want to play according to *LA Law* take the first flight to California and get on with it. Those who retain faith in the idea of a native, rooted drama have a tough fight ahead; but we have more allies than perhaps we imagine, and the most powerful of these is the audience.

Consider films as diverse as *Gregory's Girl*, *Cinema Paradiso*, *Jean de Florette* and *My Life as a Dog*. Their combined production and publicity budgets, alongside the average *SuperBatmanRobocop* movie, probably totalled about fourpence, but they found their audience and, with a long shelf life guaranteed, will continue to do so. *Their common factor is that they are specific and regional, but totally universal.* That quality – the universal in the particular – is the core of all drama that matters a damn, whether you live on the banks of the Tyne or the Tiber, and whether you are playmaker or spectator.

If we are to continue to tell our tales, an element of local control is vital. A wise man once told me that the Industrial Revolution turned sour on Tyneside when the great innovators like Stephenson were no longer able to finance their own inventions and had to rely on the City of London. There is little compassion in the average pound or dollar. By the same token, you may walk the length and breadth of the largest retail complex in Western Europe without finding the man who owns any of the stores.

The trick is to sneak under the fence while nobody is looking. If the world's media are controlled by four, or even forty men, they will be much too busy rotating their assets and building pyramids to notice the growth of a theatrical tradition or even a film industry in a distant North-East. Small is not only beautiful; it has the ability to flourish undetected.

The process is already under way. The Live Theatre Company, started in 1972 and based on Newcastle's Quayside, has provided a lively springboard for the plays of Cecil Taylor, Tom Hadaway, Leonard Barras, Phil Woods, Michael Chaplin and this author, and for dozens of actors, including Tim Healy and Kevin Whateley. The effect has been to create a pool of talent lapping over into many areas. Tyne Tees Television, BBC North-East and Amber Films have all been beneficiaries, and vice versa: it is a mutual aid community. Live Theatre is not the only example, but it is one I am familiar with, and, very properly, I feel affection and loyalty for the company. There is no serious money in it for anyone but, as Orwell pointed out, it's a pretty fair bet that if something doesn't pay, it's probably all right.

Historically, the changes over the last fifty years or so have been startling and a little scary. In the 1930s and 1940s, the perceived image of the North-East was, in effect, an angry essay by J. B. Priestley illustrated by Bill Brandt's photographs, and probably published in *Picture Post*. There might be an occasional item on Movietone News about a ship launch or a royal visit. And that was about it. Even our comedians rarely played south of Middlesbrough. It is a long journey from the Jarrow Crusade to Jimmy Nail as Spender, investigating mayhem among the yuppies.

In his autobiography, Peter Nichols defines drama as 'dreams made useful'. Much of our present confusion springs from simple ignorance of this truth. The television industry is in thrall to the advertising executives, the marketing consultants and the dealmakers. These people design the package then instruct the writer to fill it with designated ingredients, guaranteeing infinite sales in the world market. In reality, it guarantees nothing of the sort, except to the extent that using your family's dates of birth will guarantee your winning the football pools.

Ultimately, we have to trust the dream. Nothing else matters. Those of us whose dreams take place in a Tyneside landscape peopled by the descendants of Harry Hotspur must work with those dreams and make them useful.

We are also realists. We do not expect total creative freedom. That has always been a myth. I have this fantasy scene from an imaginary film about Michelangelo, as he receives his brief for the painting of the Sistine Chapel. It runs:

'We would like you to paint the ceiling of the chapel. You may paint anything you like. Draw as deeply as you wish upon the deep well of your imagination ...'

[Michelangelo cannot believe this prospect of total artistic freedom. The spokesman continues:]

'... anything you like. *Providing* it is to the greater glory of God.'

The gods change, but the principle endureth for ever. The professional writer cannot live without patronage; at best this will be a constraint, at worst it will mean censorship and imprisonment. The results need not be catastrophic. Marble is a cumbersome and inflexible building material, but the Greeks made the Parthenon with it, and, as Sartre pointed out, there is no terror like the terror of absolute freedom. Total artistic freedom is a myth, and I'm not sure we could handle it even if it were on offer.

On the whole, born as we are from generations of disenfranchised voices, Geordie writers live easily enough with this ragbag of realities. The mere fact that we are able to write and see our work performed, without being in hock to the Bloomsbury/Oxbridge axis, is awesome enough. On the whole, we are not cursed with Art in the Head. We see ourselves as *makers*, conscientious craftsmen who happen to be writers, just as our fathers happened to be railwaymen, shipbuilders or pitmen. Maybe our greatest fault is an excess of humility; we might inherit social and political rage, but along with it there's residual forelock-touching too.

What we share, to borrow an idea from Sid Chaplin, is love of place and love of work. The shipyards and the coalfield, hideous as the conditions were, nevertheless created a lasting respect for the craft tradition, linked to the notion of community interdependence: at its most trivial, borrowing a cup of sugar; at its most profound, sharing the pain of bereavement. Both of these traditions have suffered grievously during the 1980s, kicked almost to death by the bovver boots of Thatcherism. What survives is the possibility of love, and that survival depends in large measure on the writers.

To end at the beginning: I learned about storytelling in the back yard of my grandparents' house in York Street, Jarrow, on those lovely days when the family gathered for a bit crack. The family tales involved a huge and diverse cast of characters, from Palmer the shipbuilder to Buchan the footballer, from Wee Ellen the agitator to Wee Georgie Wood the comedian. When I helped Sid Chaplin and Alex Glasgow in the making of *Close The Coalhouse Door*, I called the grandparents in the play Thomas and Mary in celebration of my grandparents. My grandfather has been in many of my plays: the gentle, dignified, mischievous, self-educated, working-class aristocrat. Heavily disguised, translated into York-shire, and given a streak of political subversion, he became Big Al of the *Beiderbecke* series. He is, I suppose, one of a range of archetypes on which I play variations – akin to a jazz musician weaving infinite patterns around the structure of a twelve-bar blues. All writers do this, including Shakespeare. Every large man in drama owes something to Falstaff and Sir Toby though, as a large man called Stan observes in my novel, *Misterioso*: 'Scratch any Falstaff and you'll find a whining little Hamlet with a lorry-load of hangups'. Stereotypes, to complete this analysis, are archetypes who have fallen into the hands of lousy writers, actors, producers and direc-tors, in any order.

Memory becomes history becomes legend, and writers are the stewards in charge of the process. In the North-East, we have long memories and a massive burden of history. Ultimately, what we do can be described but not explained. We experience the poetic insights of Tom Hadaway, the surreal flights of Leonard Barras, the magisterial vision of Sid Chaplin. We wonder at their diversity but sense something in common, and the common factor is, I suggest, a memory of tales told, figuratively anyway, in the back yard. According to Sid's account, many of them were told at the coal face: Leonard has referred to falling off the fender-box laugh-ing at his uncle's stories; and Tom, I imagine, gathered much of his material around the North Shields fish quay. But the principle holds good: an oral tradition, starting in childhood, hardened by inherited rage and love.

All drama examines the same eternal questions: who are we, how did we get here and where are we going tomorrow? The early 1990s is a fascinating time to address the question 'where does North-East drama go tomorrow?' There are winds of change blowing in all directions, from Europe and elsewhere.

Among the writers, there seems to be a growing awareness that talking to ourselves about ourselves is no longer enough. In the 1960s, an onstage character saying 'Howay' was enough of a novelty to get a laugh without further embellishment. 'Howay' is no longer enough, and it's interesting to note that Tom Hadaway's most recent play, *Long Shadows*, succeeded brilliantly in taking on the mind-shredding complexities of the Middle-East situation with a company of six actors on the tiny stage at Live Theatre – but it did so from a North-East perspective. My own play, *Going Home*, presented by the same team in the North-East over the winter of 1990-1, looked at the Tyneside memory in relation to white Australia, black American jazz and Aboriginal dream time.

The cute moral: today Whitley Bay, tomorrow the world.

The serious question: when the earth is girdled with satellites and babies are implanted with cable receivers at birth, what sort of stories should we tell each other?

The serious answer: our stories should be dream-driven, not market-driven, and they should be stories that in one form or another were first heard in a back yard, once upon a time.

CHAPTER FIVE
Comic Dialect

TOM HADAWAY

IN THE NORTHUMBRIAN FILM *Seacoal*, a working woman perceives injustice:

> 'So, A've gorra 'boot an 'oor, 'cos ye've gorra gi' the gallowa' a spell ... thanks a lot.'

The Commissioning Editor for Channel Four was stunned. What on earth was the actress saying?

> 'So, I have about an hour to spare, because you have to rest the horse ... thank you very much.' 'Then why couldn't she just say exactly that?'
> ''Cos mister she'd be stood oot like a sore thumb. How aboot subtitles?'

A language within a language, dialect is the community short-hand. Not itself necessarily comic, though it may seem so to the outsider, what it mainly allows is spontaneity; direct, forceful, and expressive. I would argue – a greater significance. (Incidentally, *Seacoal* took first prize at the Munich International Film Festival.)

First, we should draw a distinction between humour contrived as 'jokes', which may be rendered in formal or sophisticated language, and that instinctive humour which is an involuntary response, only a degree away from the pain it might be denying. The ensuing laughter is a form of optimism. In this respect, 'Geordie' humour seems particularly stubborn, and therefore hopeful, but all humour best prospers in the soil to which it is native.

No doubt something desolate and in the mood of hailstones made our Viking forbears smile as they enjoyed rowing something not much larger than a fish box over the North Sea. We have retained their vowels, sullen as thunder.

'Wor Baal!' howl the football terraces of Tyneside, all cow-horned, and bristling with spears.

'Our ball!' would be an embarrassing reduction of the challenge.

Like some invocation of a pagan god, 'Wor Baal!' is much more intimidatory. If there is a joke, it is of course the referee, surrendering his faith in impartiality. However, it is not just how they are told, but that they can be told at all, for if our betters shame us out of our phrases and pronunciation, we shall be without resource. From a shared history, dialect is the enabling power of the commoner.

In a gem from Sirkka-Liisa Konttinen's *Byker*, a disapproving woman directs the stranger to a neighbour's door:

'Ye cannit miss it pet, it's the ownly dorty step in the street.'

This is not meant to be comical, and it is not a matter of form; rather it arises freely from her soul. This Byker woman would lose her punitive edge if she had to stop and think about saying:

'You are sure to notice it dear, it is the only unwashed step in the street.'

Which is only nearly as funny, for the potency of humour is immediacy, which her dialect allows, being as natural to her as gorse and thistle to a Northumbrian hillside.

I have this feeling that perhaps it is futile attempting to analyse humour, as it is a condition of tribe, and taste, but if such conversational repartee is a specific, I could leave you with 'me' Uncle George:

'A'll tell ye summick for nowt.'

He was always telling me things for 'nowt'.

'Ye'll nivvor yuk [hook] a haddock wirra pen nib' (see Figure 5.1).

Being a coble fisherman out of Cullercoats, and without benefit from his schooldays, he was given to saying disparaging things about the nature of education. 'Me' Aunty Mabel, on the other hand, would say disparaging things about 'me' Uncle George:

FIGURE 5.1: '"Ye'll nivvor yuk a haddock wirra pen nib."' *Thomas Street School, Sunderland* (1905), Photograph: Newcastle upon Tyne Libraries and Arts.

'Tek nee notice son, it's aal the years on a' open deck. The wind! It's scattered 'is brains.'

And while I am entertaining this vision of little particles of brain streaming from his leeward 'lug', she went on:

'Ee stick in at yor readin' an' writin', that's yor place on the bus. Yor chance ti mix wi' berra people.'

So here I am writing an article for a university press, but there was, and still is, a conflict of loyalty.

'Thor's nowt wrang wi' me Uncle George.'

'Thor's nowt wrang wi' donkeys son, but the' divven lerrim on buses.'

This was the woman who once devastated a customer unduly hesitating over the purchase of a crab:

'Norra grand piana y' knaa. Ownly a crab! Yor not ganna live wirrit.'

Thirty years later, my family are still laughing at the memory, but can we expect others to find it funny?

Then of course I loved them both.

So, I have a problem writing this, for there is a sense in which the term 'Comic Dialect' is an affront. It is as though it were a straying from the path, a kind of rustic frailty, funny because it is the vocabulary of idiots, and therefore where 'proper' English words exist there is no justification for it.

Entertainers expecting an audience to fall about with the mere letting slip of 'clarty', or 'marra', contribute to this feeling of offence, for language is power, and having our dialect tolerated as merely amusing is one way of rendering us powerless – one way of denying us a share. Reciting like parrots the standard texts, and trying to emulate establishment speech, plants the bulk of us firmly and mutely into the fourth division.

'The dumb go down in history', wisely observes Tony Harrison, who lives in the two worlds of 'Them and Uz'. Deploring the actors' 'neutral voice', he reproaches them for 'giving up the quality that first made them actors', and, answering those who prevail upon him to leave behind his own worlds of dropped aitches, 'How can you kick away the ladder?'

For those of us still on the bottom rungs with the need to be given the little honour of being recognised, comic dialect has a serious purpose.

'The boss would like to see you, Smith.'

'Wassa marra, is 'e gannin' blind?'

Sometimes we have to puncture the bladders of pomposity.

Then sometimes it is about having a clearer perspective. This 'favourite', overheard on Wallsend High Street, is an elderly lady shopper reflecting on a visit to the Metro shopping centre.

'Wor Betty's man run us ower. Hev ye not been? Like a palace ... foontins, plants, ... aal spotless! Band playin' while ye get yor coffee. Loads o' stuff. Gans for miles. Just aboot ivvorythin' ye cud think on! Naw! A didn't buy nowt. Couldn't see owt A needed!'

Smile a little at 'Wor Betty's man run us ower' for its suggestion of a traffic victim – but we must not permit ourselves indulgent, amused superiority by regarding this woman as a bit of a character, a quaintly-spoken comic oddity. For she is a tremendous speaker. With the phrase 'Couldn't see owt A needed', she has subconsciously, but powerfully, stubbed a finger of scorn at consumerism. Her wry, discerning and withering irony, lost to the professional writer or the polemicist, is available to her through instinct and dialect, and is a sure indication of the genius in nature that flourishes exuberant and humorous in those who have not been educated out of their minds. She is the robust and eternal. Before Bede, before Dr Johnson and his first English dictionary, she was here, rich, commanding and revelatory, and she will be around speaking in her splendid terms when their pages have yellowed. For it is the strength and endurance of dialect that it is regenerative and innovatory, fulfilling the need of humanity for a voice in an ever-changing world.

'Bugga aal money me! but A'm hard', cries the strident Geordie youth facing his modern dilemma, where once the colliery stood, and the 'cavils', 'cundies' and 'netties' of his 'da' are grassed over.

Suddenly it all sounds more disturbing, vulgar and aggressive, and all those dire things they warned us of at 'skeul', about using language like 'Had yor gob', or 'Clout yor lug'. But the purpose is the same, for dialect is not merely sometimes, but always and forever about defiance. The recognition of this by Shaw, and the editor of *Viz*, brings the huge success of Eliza Doolittle and of the Fat Slags. It is not that they are enormously funny, but that they are enormously irreverent.

Those Fat Slags, they must have come ashore with the Vikings. Cursing like sleet, blackening the buds, raging at the monk of Jarrow scribbling his morality and judgement into a book (see Figure 5.2), their scorn for linguistic and social propriety may shock, endear or outrage, but it cannot be ignored.

Of course, there are problems of access and understanding. Concessions need to be made. Then let 'Them' make them. There are more of 'Uz'. Do they not know what rewards, discoveries and gains await, even in ... incomprehension?

'This play has suffered in travelling', said the *Telegraph* (The Monte Carlo International Television Festival, 1975), 'depending upon its rugged language, which failed to impress the judges.' There had been this line: 'Gan ti Ann, an' tell hor A'll torn' – being a Northumbrian pitman's offer to change his religion, but dubbed into French it had somehow come out:

'Allez-vous à Ann, and tell her I am revolving' (see Figure 5.3).

Come on! They must have had a laugh.

Don't they know what they are missing? Comic dialect! Is it not the inheritance? The sacred grove wherein imagination fruits. The rich vein, the knot, and bond, and bringing together of the tribe. The liberation of their wit for the consolation of dark days, or the lustre and increase of their hopes and dreams.

Don't they realise the price they pay, who travel sleek but lonely in the padded exile of BMW or Jag, not to be able to share in the peal of public laughter that greets

'Scuse me! Duz this bus stop on the Quay?'
'It bloody well berra hinny!'

Don't they feel deprived? Then with what joy to see a traveller's return.

This week in the *Newcastle Journal*, its music critic reviewed the Scottish National Opera's production of Verdi at the Theatre Royal. His fine, intelligent prose was so erudite you had to read it twice. 'Showing the greatest range of timbre . . .', 'Subtlety of vocal

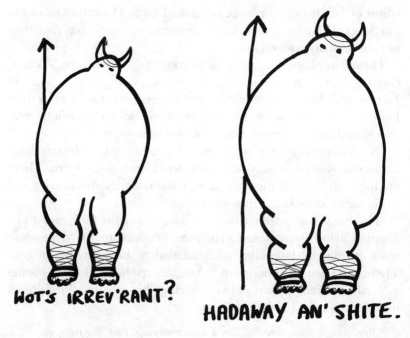

FIGURE 5.2: 'Cursing like sleet, blackening the buds, raging at the monk of Jarrow scribbling his morality and judgement into a book.'

FIGURE 5.3: '"Allez-vous à Ann, and tell her I am revolving."' *Girl with Hula-Hoop* (1957), Photograph: courtesy of Jimmy Forsyth and West Newcastle Local Studies Centre (from *Scotswood Road*, Bloodaxe Books, 1986).

interpretation . . .'; but then, hunting in his head for a suitable term to express his one disappointment, added:

But the chorus seemed clagged on.

I think his name was Kevin. Oh! well done Kevin, bonny lad! Brilliant! Inspired! You have listened to yor da and yor ma and it has robed you with destiny.

CHAPTER SIX

'Keep Your Feet Still, Geordie Hinnie'
Women and Work on Tyneside

ELAINE KNOX

THE CONURBATION OF TYNESIDE was shaped by geographic circumstance, economic prerogatives and the industrial development and
demands of the nineteenth century. A heartland of the Industrial
Revolution, its historical, industrial and social development
stemmed from its position on the Northern coalfield and its position
around the Tyne estuary. The shaping of Tyneside's identity was
impelled by the dominance of the five great staple industries that
emerged in the nineteenth century and attained not only regional
dominance but also national importance. Coalmining and export,
shipping, shipbuilding, iron production and heavy engineering
determined the region's economic health, its social condition and
make-up until their final collapse in the 1970s and 1980s, but their
legacy has continued long after their real economic dominance, in
terms of employment, declined.

Their remarkable expansion and success, especially during the
second half of the nineteenth century, absorbed the bulk of the
region's labour force. Their workplace organisation and the values
derived from it helped shape a distinctive sense of regional identity.
The wage packet, and how and where that wage packet was earned,
played a major part in the development of Tyneside's cultural and
social ethos.

Tyneside's predominantly working-class population and relatively small middle class, in which the ratio of the sexes was

balanced, together with a marriage rate well above the national average and a larger-than-average family size, encouraged a social and community structure strongly centred around work, the family and local community. This, combined with a strong sense of regional identity and fierce pride in the region's economic achievements, produced a highly distinctive regional outlook.

A regional economy dependent on heavy industries and employing mainly male labour went hand in hand with an enthusiastic consensus adoption and approval of the Victorian domestic model – the man as breadwinner, and the woman as wife and mother, working in the clearly defined and separate spheres of home and workplace. Moreover, the demands made on women in servicing men bound to a cycle of heavy industrial work, and the comparatively high wages earned in shipyard, foundry and mine during their expansionist years, reinforced the separation of women from a waged economic role outside the home.

Economic concentration of Tyneside's industrial eggs in five interdependent baskets led to a narrowing of the region's industrial base and allowed few visible large-scale openings for women to work. The higher profits and higher wages offered during the expansionist years absorbed regional capital investment, entrepreneurial management and skilled labour. Older industries such as saltmaking, glass manufacture, pottery manufacture, papermaking, carpeting and hatmaking – employing both men and women – stagnated and declined. Small-scale textile industries could not compete against the large-scale, modernised industries in other regions without heavy investment and modernised equipment.

By the turn of the century, the idea that 'women didn't work' had become an established social tenet and a community ideal. It would hold good for the next sixty years, shaping perceptions of the region's identity and its history. This economic marginalisation of women led to their social marginalisation. Political, social and leisure institutions would develop around waged work and reinforce this. Women would be debarred from the pub and the club and excluded from the majority of union and Labour Party activities, and 'leisure' would become the prerogative of the working man.

Considering the North-East's historic contribution to the national economy, there have been remarkably few histories of the region. The modern history of Tyneside tends to be a history of industry, work, employment and unemployment. This is, however, a history perceived through male work, masculine employment and a male workforce. There have been more words written on the geological formation of the Northern coalfield than on women's part in regional life. It would be pardonable to ask 'were there any women on Tyneside?' (see Figure 6.1).

What historical record there is has been confined to women's role as domestic victims – the powerless sufferers of social conditions, mere ciphers used to illustrate the state of the region's health, education and sanitary conditions. In the spate of works written in the 1930s, women serve as examples illustrating the social evils caused by male unemployment, suffering through their role as wife and mother, domestic manager and servicer of the labour force, and ascribed no economic role of their own. As a result, much of women's waged work has gone unrecorded and unrecognised. The documentary evidence of women's working past has been lost or destroyed, or, in many cases, assigned so little importance that

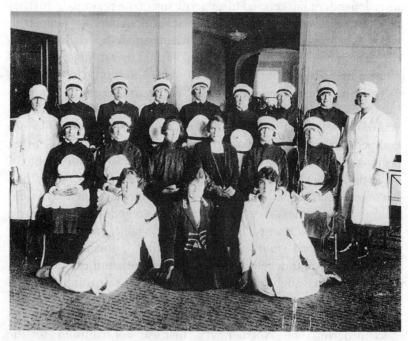

FIGURE 6.1: 'There have been more words written on the geological formation of the Northern coalfield than on women's part in regional life. It would be pardonable to ask "were there any women on Tyneside?"' *Tilley's, Blackett Street, Newcastle* (1920s), Photograph: Newcastle upon Tyne Libraries and Arts.

records were not kept. In the region's local history rooms and archives, those company and workplace records that do survive are rarely indexed or given prominence as 'women's work', in dramatic contrast to the North-West, with its long tradition of a large-scale, highly visible female workforce. Work, leisure, union activity and protest form the single-gender lens through which the past is viewed. One half of the region's population has been omitted from its history because of the assumption that women played no significant economic role. Yet to a large extent this assumption is as much a product of cultural mythology as economic fact.

The interwar years are especially indicative of the elements that have rendered women's work on Tyneside invisible. In the nineteenth century, the focus of regional history was the celebration of industrial production. Output, shipping tonnage and the praising of the commercial enterprises of great Northern entrepreneurs shaped the eulogies. However, the collapse of the major industries and the onset of mass unemployment brought a new approach. At a time when the social and political implications of mass unemployment dominated the political agenda and popular press, Tyneside moved from major producer to economic cripple. A series of reports, commencing with H. A. Mess's *Industrial Tyneside* in 1928 and culminating in the 1934-8 government reports on depressed regions, introduced planned regional policy programmes. The region would remain tagged as a 'Distressed Area' until political expediency and the Conservative government ideology of the 1980s, rather than economic recovery, would remove it. The impact of the Depression was of lasting significance. It is still strongly influential in shaping the nation's view of Tyneside and Tynesiders.

The Depression brought in its wake a flurry of officially sponsored and conducted reports, and a wandering troop of writers and journalists flocked to observe the suffering. It also saw the first tentative beginnings of a regional policy. In a region where sixty-four per cent of the workforce relied on five heavy industries, the impact of mass unemployment in the big five was intensified.

Women made brief appearances as social victims. Although there is a wealth of detailed descriptions available for the 1920s and 1930s, it is an analysis of male occupations, of male employment and unemployment and its social and psychological impact on men. Indeed, the very word 'unemployment' is given a strongly masculine identity. Once again, women remained firmly excluded as significant participants in the region's labour force.

The impact of the Depression years provided a new set of symbols and images and a cultural legacy that would survive to the present. Images of men standing visibly idle in the streets, or queues seeking work outside factory gates, or pinched, half-starved faces waiting outside the labour exchanges, despairing groups playing pitch-and-toss on street corners and the stolid desperation and pride of the Jarrow marchers became a standard currency of description. G. Fenner Brockway, for example, observed in *Hungry England* (1932)

> a block of men. Two hundred of them I should think, standing eight in a line. . . . I see a solid mass of grey clothes, black mufflers, cloth caps.

The whole of Tyneside became homogeneous with Jarrow, an industrial wasteland populated by unemployed gangs of shipyard workers.

A kind of standardised vocabulary of unemployment and associated images developed – a cultural yardstick to measure other recessions by. The same descriptions, the same sentences, phrases and images deriving from the 1930s reappeared in the 1970s. And it is a vocabulary that excludes women (see Figure 6.2). Women are simply not perceived as 'unemployed' because they do not fit into the standardised conceptions of unemployment. Employment and unemployment are categorised through 'visibility'. Men are perceived as having one main role, that of breadwinner and worker, central to their lives. Dislocated from work, they become visibly helpless, workless and, divorced from their primary role as breadwinner, socially alienated and adrift. Men, if not seen working, are assumed to be 'unemployed'. Women are simply not expected to be seen working at all.

Tyneside's heavy industries employed large workforces, physically concentrated, with clearly defined 'work' and 'leisure' boundaries within distinctive locations – the factory, the shipyard, the pit and the pub. Women's work time and leisure time did not fall within these boundaries. Unemployed women are not visible; they simply slip back into the boundaries of the home role. They become invisible. They do not hang around street corners in large, idle groups. The streets and back lanes of Tyneside were the women's domain: they ran the street networks and were rarely seen to be idle

FIGURE 6.2: 'The same descriptions, the same sentences, phrases and images deriving from the 1930s reappeared in the 1970s. And it is a vocabulary that excludes women.' *Ellen Wilkinson MP* (1936), Photograph: South Tyneside Libraries.

or standing around doing 'nothing'. When Fenner Brockway visited Tyneside, he was appalled by the large groups of men standing around the street, the massive queues of men outside the 'dole', patiently doing nothing, their very presence on the street and outside their houses during 'work time' stating their unemployment. He was surprised to find that the Public Assistance Committee member he was to interview was female:

> An hour ago when I went through the streets, I noticed only the men. Now I see the women. At house after house they are busy cleaning windows, polishing doorknobs. The PAC (Public Assistance Committee) member we are seeking is a woman, and we find her at the general task. She stands on the pavement, with pail by her side, scrubbing the windowsill.

In a region where fewer than twenty per cent of women worked, the problem of female unemployment was rated as being of low concern. This attitude persisted well into the 1960s and 1970s, disguising the fact that by 1970 some forty per cent of the regional workforce were women. By the 1970s, working women had become the major element of growth in the local economy, falling in line with the national average. Moreover, the major part of the female workforce was made up from married women – in marked contrast to the predominantly single workforce of the first half of the century.

The low priority of women's work in the first half of the century was clearly reflected in the work of the labour exchange-appointed Employment Committees. According to both census sources and the Employment Exchange returns, the major occupations employing women were domestic service and personal service – which included barmaids, laundrywomen and inns and hotels – as well as shop assistants, clerks and typists, dressmakers, tailoresses and professional workers (mainly teachers and nurses). The bulk of these occupations (with the exception of teaching), with their predominantly female workforces, were perceived as 'feminised', suitable for women but not for men, with lower wages and little chance of promotion or advancement. Because these occupations came to be seen as 'women's work', there were few efforts made either to promote them or, in the case of trade unionism, to promote higher wages. Higher wages for male workers, the 'natural' bread-winners, were enshrined in government legislation and union expectations. Indeed, the tendency to see women workers as a threat to pay and work conditions – their inclusion leading to dilution and de-skilling – was intensified on Tyneside. In a region proud of its union affiliations, and with the dominance of the highly masculinised and skilled unions of shipyard and engineering factory and the all-male membership of mining and seafaring unions fighting pay battles on the grounds of 'family', levels of pay and the problem of female unemployment received short shrift.

Measures aimed at alleviating unemployment were aimed primarily at men. The only group of women to merit any degree of attention were single women, and such measures looked no further than existing regional employment patterns. 'Girls' were simply pushed into the traditional catch-all of domestic service. The Employment Committees' public statements, alongside those of the Department of Labour, stressed both the success of these measures and the limited aspirations behind them. Many of the measures were aimed at transferring northern girls to those areas in the south with shortages of domestic labour. Captain Euan Wallace, appointed by the government to tour and report on the worst unemployment blackspots, reported that by 1934 some 9,807 girls had trained at the Domestic Training Centres in the North-East and that only 1.9 per cent of them were still registered as unemployed. A private organisation, run by Mrs Cuthbert Headlam, had successfully transferred a further 7,000 women to other parts of the country. Such 'successes' were widely praised:

> Durham girls have now acquired such an excellent reputation as domestic servants that the demand exceeds the supply, and in some villages it has been found that almost every girl over the age of 15 has left the village and found employment elsewhere.
>
> (Reports of Investigations into the Industrial Conditions in Certain Depressed Areas, 1934)

Privately, the authorities acknowledged that domestic service was unpopular. Girls and women had to be coerced by the threat of removal of benefits into attending the courses and entering the transferral schemes. Throughout the 1920s and 1930s, they struggled with a succession of cases where women undergoing training refused to undertake residential domestic work. Such refuseniks were called before the Committees, and claims made on grounds of sickness or domestic commitments were closely scrutinised. Moreover, domestic service was not covered under National Insurance. Women from other occupations who had paid into the scheme lost their entitlement to benefit if they took up work in service. Understandably, this increased the unpopularity of domestic service compared with other forms of paid work. Beyond domestic training, there was little other training provision made for women. Attempts at relief for the unemployed, organised through the Tyneside Bureau for Social Services or Local Authority relief schemes, were mainly aimed at men. The only provision for women lay in sewing, soft-furnishing and cookery classes. These were aimed chiefly at the wives of unemployed men, and no attempt was made to provide training in non-domestic occupations.

How well founded these public proclamations of success in dealing with women's unemployment were is debatable. It is no coincidence that the *Shields Gazette* began to run a new cartoon series, 'Millie the Maid', in the 1930s, just at a time when domestic service was becoming increasingly unpopular. Private recollections of life in service stressed the hard physical labour, the lack of freedom, and the low wages and humiliations inflicted upon domestic

servants. Millie was depicted as a blonde and amiable flibbertigibbet, cosily ensconced in a small, middle-class family. On the best of
terms with 'Mum', and rarely depicted as lifting anything heavier
than a duster or plate of biscuits, Millie's endeavours bore little
relation to reality.

The Employment Exchange Committee's members shared little
empathy with working women. Predominantly middle-class and
formed from employers, unions and the occasional 'women's' representative, they had little real understanding of the realities of
women's lives. At North Shields, one Committee reputedly dealt
with several unemployed women by sending them to work at a local
'cafe' – blissfully unaware that it was in reality a brothel. Faced
with recalcitrant or 'difficult' women (mainly those unable or
unwilling to enter training or transferral schemes), they wrote them
off as 'unsuitable' or of the 'factory type'.

Provisions for married women's work were virtually non-
existent. Those older or married women registered with exchanges
proved particularly problematic. The only areas explored by the
Committees involved efforts to increase the number of char-
women's jobs available. Married working women were seen as
strange and unfamiliar, a problem that did not belong to this area,
although the concept of large numbers of women working in Lancashire was familiar to Committee members. The idea of married
women working outside the home was actively disapproved of, by
both working-class and middle-class members. As one member of
the Committee remarked:

> Most of the women locally on becoming married were fully aware that
> they would not be able to continue in industrial employment and
> probably every member of the Committee would agree that unless a
> woman showed evidence, on marriage, of continuing in employment
> she should be regarded as outside the scope of Unemployment
> Insurance.

Both official assessments and public perceptions of employment
presented some interesting anomalies. Despite the general assumptions of industrial collapse, and despite mass unemployment, there
were some growth areas. There are notable differences between the
bleak picture of male unemployment and the developing sectors of
women's employment in wholesale and retail dealing and public
services.

Against the general background of gloom, shop work and retail flourished, with an increasingly feminised workforce. Indeed, per-capita expenditure increased. Jarrow may have been stricken and its corner shops bereft of custom, but the Co-op expanded in the teeth of the Depression. There was a striking contrast between the new, glossy department and chain store premises and the family run, smaller shop. The roots of the postwar retailing revolution lay in the 1930s. C&A Modes and British Home Stores both opened in Newcastle. Fenwick's expanded, but did not need to recruit through the labour exchanges. The corner shop had long been the popular dream of the working-class man and woman. Faced with hardship, many a family's first resource was to open up part of the house as a small shop. The small-scale making and selling of cakes, pies and small-scale groceries had long been the preserve of women, allowing them to contribute money to the household budget yet combine work with home and the family. There are no accurate assessments of how many of these shops were in existence, and frequently they were started and run by wives, yet registered in the husband's name.

Similarly, that first resort of the financially desperate woman without capital enough for shopkeeping or hawking remained laun-drywork. A 'respectable' option for the impoverished widow, the hard-up wife or the woman who could not work outside the home, and especially prevalent in dockside economies, such work passed unnoticed and invisible. At the other end of the scale, the newly rationalised and large-scale modernised laundries such as Harton Cleaners employed large numbers of women throughout Tyneside. A whole submerged economy operated, casually, informally and with fluid boundaries, where women could slip into wages work and out again, back to the domestic duties of the home. A flourish-ing band of penny capitalists existed out of, and beneath, official notice. In an area where the male death rate was high and where in towns such as North Shields and South Shields some one in seven were employed in shipping and with trips of up to two and three years at sea common, cultural tenets against waged work could prove more fluid and elastic than hindsight allowed, and economic necessity overran or slipped round social restrictions.

Since the official preoccupation was with male employment, female employment went uncounted. It was a regional tendency that marginalised those smaller growth industries that would fuel postwar growth. The whole of the female workforce, both actual and potential, was dismissed as insignificant:

> It [the manufacture of domestic goods for home consumption] has brought with it greater opportunities for women in industry, in itself an excellent thing, but taken with the decline in male employment it means a net reduction in the Area's contribution to the economic wealth of the nation. In our view it is highly improbable that any expansion of these industries and services can take place on such a scale as to make up for a continued loss in the heavy industries for which the Area is so favourably situated.
> (HMSO, An Industrial Survey of the North-East Coast Area, 1932)

The report concluded that:

> The potential supply of women and girls is so considerably in excess of both the present and future demand that any estimate would be as useless as it is difficult.

Even when the number of working women soared from the 1950s onwards, it was dismissed. The grip of the past ensured working women's invisibility. One striking feature was the fear that this growth inspired. It was seen either as an irritating hiccup in regional growth and planning, or as a threat to the need to place the rising numbers of redundant miners and shipyard workers. There were few efforts to promote or control the growing 'feminised' industries, or to encourage better conditions in the service industries that would provide the bulk of postwar growth.

One factor that made a major contribution to this marginalisation lay in how the labour force was calculated – notably from census returns and from insured work statistics, obtained via the labour exchanges. It is questionable whether either source provided a reliable means of assessing or measuring women's work in the region. Both relied heavily on what women (and their husbands) perceived as 'waged work'. A striking feature of oral evidence is how variable were perceptions of what was and what was not 'waged work'. On Tyneside, the concept of 'work' draws heavily on the legacy of the past. Local symbols and icons, the 'big hewer' 'Geordie and his marra' – hard, muscled men doing hard physical labour – formed the role models. Men in shipyards, men in docks; sweat, sinew and muck shaped local conceptions.

'Real' work was considered to be welding, hewing, quarrying, smelting and shaping. It had highly physical, even sexual, overtones. This was especially true for a predominantly working-class population whose work values predominated and shaped its cultural and social values. The ability to work, and the type of work done, formed an integral part of entry into 'manhood'. Work, masculinity and a man's position in house and community as the family breadwinner were inextricably linked to men's self-evaluation. 'Real work', the qualities imbued in that work and the qualities and virtues of those carrying out that work were firmly masculinised, as were the structures and social activities around work. Conversely, domestic work, the labour of caring and servicing home and family, was feminised and separated from the economic world of waged work. To transgress these boundaries and to clash with these social normatives was to expose men to the risk of being classified as effeminate. Similarly, a woman stepping outside these values through waged work became defeminised and unwomanly, risking her social standing as a woman in kin and community networks and damaging her evaluation as a wife and mother. On Tyneside, occupations tended to fall firmly within these masculine or feminine categories. This single-gender appropriation of 'real work' and its associated concepts – skills, craftsmanship, training, the pay packet with all its connotations of earned leisure and status – was central to Tyneside culture. The classification of occupations and modes of production as 'masculine' or 'feminine' played (and still plays) a key role in shaping gender-specific patterns of work, work expectations, conditions and pay. Paul Willis has noted, in *Working-Class Culture* (1979):

> A trade is judged not for itself, nor even for its great financial return, but for its ability to provide the central, domestic role for its incumbent. Clearly money is part of this – but as a means not the essence. ... The male wage packet is held to be central, not simply because of its size, but because it is won in a masculine mode in confrontation with the 'real' world which is too tough for the women. Thus the man in the domestic household is held to be the bread-winner, 'the worker', while the wife works for the extras. Very often of course, the material importance of her wage may be much greater than this suggests, and certainly her domestic labour is the lynchpin [sic] of the whole household economy. The wage packet as a kind of symbol of machismo dictates the domestic culture and economy and tyrannises both men and women.

Women's work frequently falls outside the categories of masculinised 'work'. The lines between men's work and home life are
clearly drawn. Much of the work available to women in the first half
of the century, and the line between it and the home, were far more
diffuse. Moreover, the primary role ascribed to women was as
housewife and mother. Many women did not think of themselves as
workers, even when they earned money through work. Casual,
part-time and seasonal waged work tended to be subsumed under
that role. Women viewed waged work through the assumptions of
the society around them, and on Tyneside these were chiefly masculine in origin. Male labour power applied to the earning of money
was seen as 'work'; female labour power exerted in the running of
the home was considered to be a natural and integral part of
women's feminine role. Men, in applying the same values to their
wives' and daughters' work, frequently failed to differentiate the
service role at home as work when transferred to outside the home
for money. The part-time barmaid, working within a traditionally
'womanly' occupation, was not necessarily classed as 'working' by
her husband. A collective desire to remain within the bounds of
'respectability' and social acceptance, and a desire not to rock the
domestic boat or show their husbands up as poor providers, further
obscured much of women's work and ensured that a communal
'blind eye' was turned to many areas of such work. Middle-class
occupations and the better-paid skilled male jobs allowed this
visible 'respectability' to be achieved through a non-working and
well-maintained wife and family. For working-class men and
women, the maintenance (or at least the apparent maintenance) of
this tradition enhanced the social status of the whole family.

The male ego was highly sensitive. The status of both the husband, and through him the wife, was given through the successful
fulfilment of the 'breadwinner' role. The differentiation between
good and bad men – masculine prowess or inadequacy – lay in how
well they provided for their family. The status of a Tyneside man
lay in the size and the regularity of his pay packet, and the manner
in which he turned a proportion of it over to his wife. From a wife's
point of view, the greater the proportion handed over, the greater
her estimation of the man. Even issues such as domestic violence
and infidelity were secondary to the matter of financial provision
and security. Drinking, a strong regional tradition, was important
in that it played a major part in when and how much of men's

wages successfully made it into the family budget. Having earned it and handed it over, his duties were fulfilled. Even the domestic threats of drinking and gambling were condoned, provided he conformed to social and domestic expectations first, and constrained them within reasonable, socially accepted levels.

The values ascribed to a woman's status were also clearly delineated. Success or failure lay in fulfilling society's expectations, and these revolved around the domestic role, excluding waged work. Successful management of the budget, and the domestic conditions she provided for her husband and family and their physical well being, formed the bulk of that role. Successful completion in the face of inadequate income and inadequate housing brought to the fore the qualities of self-sacrifice, forbearance and self-denial that became vital elements of women's respectability. While these qualities were central to working-class culture nationally, on Tyneside, a region where community and family values were especially emphasised and which suffered economic depression and high levels of unemployment throughout the century, they were special. The physical and psychological needs of working men were expected to be paramount. Fulfilling these needs did, and was expected to, take up the whole of a woman's day. Not for her the fruits and compensations of waged work – the right to drink, amuse oneself, gamble or simply relax. A working married woman was probably a shirking woman, neglecting her duties at home. The 'dinner on the table' ethic was central to, and symbolic of, women's respectability.

Women themselves tended to be less likely to ascribe to themselves a strong work or occupational identity. They were less likely to work for long periods within a particular category of work, or for one industry or firm. The sheer fluidity of women's movement from job to job, or between the domestic and the economic role, blurs identification with a single, highly defined work identity as demanded by official categories and the census. Moreover, women's choice of work, and their expectations and aspirations through work, operated along very different lines from those of men. Convenience and ability to fit work around family commitments headed the list of priorities, while men put wages and promotion prospects first. Additionally, women's recruitment tended to be conducted along different lines. Women relied far more on word of mouth, or community and kinship networks, in seeking and securing work. Even in those large industries employing women, such as the ropeworks, the potteries and the herring industry, recruitment tended to be informal, based around the factory gates, thus further reducing official recognition of women's working role.

Oral evidence strongly reinforces the idea that official records grossly underestimated the extent and nature of women's work. It also brings to prominence those industries which figured most strongly in women's collective work-consciousness, usually those that offered the best employment opportunities, but which were ascribed little importance. Those which employed married women figured particularly – firms like Crawford's Biscuits at South Shields and the Tyne Brand factory at North Shields, that ran 'twilight shifts' which could be fitted around family commitments, or the smokehouses and herring industry at North Shields which operated on a seasonal cycle. Reyrolles Engineering was fondly and frequently recalled by many interviewees, noted not just for the large numbers of women that passed through, often working there for a relatively short period of time, but also for the relatively good wages, the friendly atmosphere and the easy-going attitude of the managers. The Co-op factories at Pelaw employed large numbers of women, and working for the Co-op was considered to have status – not matched by the wages. The opening of Team Valley in 1937 afforded new opportunities for work. With the exception of Hood Haggie's ropeworks, which occupied a particularly prominent place in community consciousness, all of these firms were expanding in the interwar years.

One of the more interesting anomalies lay in how many of these industries were popularly perceived. Francie Nichol gives a graphic description of how fluid and easily accessible employment around the herring industry was. Employing some 2,600, rising to 5,000 in the season, the fish quay formed a focus for women workers in both North and South Shields. 'Broken' herrings could be bought cheaply, and the only equipment needed was a basket or board and a knife. Barrows could also be hired by the day. North Shields market also provided fruit and vegetables that could be hawked alongside fish and shellfish. The work was hard, dirty and physical. However, although low-status and 'dirty' work, it was easily accessible, regardless of marital status.

The ropeworks fulfilled a similar function. Dirty, arduous work, physically demanding and requiring a certain degree of skill, it was well paid, even if low-status. Nicknamed 'Haggie's Angels', the ropeworkers, however, were accorded a high degree of notoriety on Tyneside. The same sort of factory-based, cultural tendencies considered natural to large, all-male workforces, when exhibited by women, were strongly condemned. In Nigel Gray's *The Worst of Times* (1985), one Tynesider recalled:

> 'Any man would do anything to get a job but there were two places they were terrified of being sent, because once you got that green card and you didn't go for the job, you didn't get any dole. One was Haggie's Ropery, North Shields. Ninety-nine per cent of them were women making these thick rope hawsers for the ships. If a man got a ticket to go for that, if they needed a man for something or other, he used to be terrified. These women were practically dehumanised because of the conditions they worked and lived under. They'd strip him and they'd probably rupture him through their frolicking.'

In popular male consciousness, ropeworkers figured as 'inhuman', and certainly unfeminine and low. They swore, they wore dirty working clothes and were alleged to drink and to be sexually free. The work-based cultural practices that were considered a natural and healthy right to male workforces were condemned when exercised by a large group of women. Perhaps because this was indubitably 'real' work, demanding physical commitment and effort in 'real work' conditions and paying comparatively high wages, it was seen as threatening. The high degree of condemnation accorded to the ropery workers may have been because of the exceptional nature of the work, as there were few highly visible, large-scale industries employing women, but it is significant that the ropery workers fulfilled all the tenets traditionally ascribed to 'masculine' work in heavy industry. Also, the manufactured end product, heavy-duty ropes supplying the shipping and mining industry, could also be regarded as 'masculine'.

The Maling pottery factory girls were not accorded the same degree of hostility. Nicknamed Maling's 'White Mice', because of the white clay dust on their boots, even the nickname implied a greater degree of respectability and respect. The Maling Ford B factory was large and highly organised, and the workforce, mainly women, were highly conscious of the skilled nature of their work. Apprenticeships varied between three years, for the jolly throwers, to five years for the gilders. The higher-paid gilders and painters, known as 'The Ladies', were accorded immense respect within the factory. The girls themselves were very aware of the value and status of apprenticeship, and proud of their work. Both the Maling women and those at the Adamsez sanitary ware factory developed very strong work-identities and a sense of satisfaction deriving from the skill needed. This contrasts quite strongly with the low priority and weak sense of identity with work exhibited by women working in a large number of places in jobs without a degree of skill, or where there were few fellow workers.

Haggie's and Maling's represented opposite ends of the factory scale in terms of public opinion and status. They also illustrate how the manufactured product played an important part in evaluating that status. The further away the product from those traditionally associated with 'men's work', and the lighter and cleaner the nature of the work, the more socially acceptable as women's work it was. The introduction of light engineering on a wider scale, and the manufacture of new consumer products, was to widen opportunities and raise the formerly low status of female factory work.

Although most North-East history, fixed firmly in the regional policy tradition, defines factory work as a postwar phenomenon, there is evidence that it had already established itself in the female consciousness from the 1920s onwards. Under the Special Areas Act of 1934, the Team Valley Corporation and the government attempted to attract newer, more diverse industries to the North-East. For the first time, a potentially large, female workforce was promoted to attract would-be employers to the region, while existing factories, such as Tyne Brand and Cremona Toffees, were promoted as proving that Tyneside's workforce could and would adapt to newer industries and that Tyneside women, given the opportunity, could and would work. The achievements of local and highly successful firms managed on efficient and modern lines, such as the Harton Laundry at South Shields, were loudly proclaimed to attract new businesses to the area. Over thirty factories were occupied on Team Valley Estate before the war, and special efforts were made to attract foreign refugees, particularly Jews with a background in light industry.

Although this policy came under considerable regional attack in the press, from the trade unions and from local councillors, with accusations of abnormally low wages, exploitation and sweating by immigrant employers, there is little direct evidence that these allegations were based on facts rather than local suspicion and jealousy. Some of the most bitter attacks were launched by people with a vested interest, or who felt that the new factories gained unfair concessions. Others expressed fears that these new factories employed too many women when the priority should be in finding work for unemployed men. Despite the popular view that factory work was 'common' or lacked respectability compared to the more 'desirable' jobs such as shop work, many women found that the higher wages and piece-work bonuses made factory work attractive.

From the 1930s onward, some aspects of women's work were being promoted and made visible, and it was even claimed that the old tenet that 'women didn't work' lay in the past:

> There has been in the past an obstacle to the establishment of light industries in the North-East. This was nothing less than the traditional pride of men-folk that they, and not their wives and daughters, were the wage-earners in the factory. One of the beneficial effects of the depression was to remove this pride and thus to release on to the labour market a large reservoir of girls, so necessary for and so popular with the lighter industries...
> (Tyneside Industrial Review, 1938)

The growth of the female workforce was to become the most important dynamic in postwar Tyneside's economic development. The major element within it has been married women working, and the expansion of what was once termed the 'secondary' service sectors. Regional history and popular perception have labelled it as a postwar phenomenon. World War II drew the women into the munitions factories and the public services, smashing the regional mould. Although the female dilutees who helped work the foundries, shipyards and engineering plants of Tyneside were firmly expelled after the war, their entry into public services, transport and telecommunications was not so easily repulsed. Tyneside's experience mirrored the national one depicted by Penny Summerfield in *Total War and Social Change* (ed. A. Marwick, 1988), and, against the region's masculine culture and economy, the impact was dramatic. After the war, the female genie would not return to her bottle (see Figure 6.3). The growth of manufacturing and light industry, and the astonishing expansion in the clerical and professional sectors, provided work for both working-class and middle-class girls. Under the regional policy umbrella, and spurred on by the decline of the mining and shipbuilding industries, strenuous efforts were made to restructure and diversify Tyneside's industrial base. While these

FIGURE 6.3: 'The growth of the female workforce was to become the most important dynamic in postwar Tyneside's economic development.... After the war, the female genie would not return to her bottle.' *Gibson's Fruit and Veg, Scotswood Road* (1958), Photograph: courtesy of Jimmy Forsyth and West Newcastle Local Studies Centre (from *Scotswood Road*, Bloodaxe Books, 1986).

policies were chiefly aimed at providing new opportunities for male employment, to a greater extent the female labour sector benefited. The new consumer industries and services were orientated towards female employment, and Tyneside's women were not as constrained as the men by the work expectations of the past. The chauvinistic culture engendered by the declining heavy industries did not turn lightly from its heritage. Tyneside men, with their family and community traditions and pride bound up in the old industries, were suspicious of the new. They offered few opportunities for displays of the hard, tough, physical qualities considered essential to 'manly' work. Their wives and daughters, without that tradition of work, were more adaptable.

The trend towards women working increased dramatically throughout the 1960s and 1970s both regionally and nationally. The establishment and growth of technical training colleges, capable of training hundreds of girls in a year to staff the counters and offices of the growing service sector, marked a quiet revolution. Work was no longer expected to be the prerogative of single girls and widows. By the 1980s, the greatest growth element in both regional and national workforces was married women entering the labour market, and not only married women, but married women with children. The two-job family and the working wife were firmly established as socially acceptable.

In 1921, only twenty-one per cent of women on Tyneside worked, compared with thirty-four per cent nationally. By the 1980s, in line with the national average, women made up forty-five per cent of the regional workforce. Yet if this growth in the number of working women was such a startling postwar phenomenon, why has Tyneside's determinedly masculine culture survived in the face of this onslaught? Surely such a radical revolt against women's traditional role would have produced a collective nervous breakdown in Tyneside's men? Why has it not been marked by dramatic domestic and cultural friction? The men of Tyneside seem to have survived this social and economic earthquake with many of their illusions intact. Role models for Andy Capp and Sid the Sexist still abound. The Little Waster is more in evidence than *Cosmopolitan*'s 'New Man'. The cartoon pages still centre around stereotyped errant husbands and nagging wives, flibbertigibbet secretaries and their lecherous, pinstriped bosses and the sort of standard bride/groom/ mother-in-law jokes that could have been safely published in the 1950s.

Despite the fact that it is women workers who staffed the retailing revolution, who made the Metro Centre and Eldon Centre possible and who celebrate their economic independence in the Bigg Market every weekend, the comfortable assumptions of the past still remain. Images of Tyneside remain those of the past. Nostalgia and regional beer adverts keep alive the comfortable, cosy images of 'Geordie' down the pub with his mates (an old-fashioned pub that you'd be hard pushed to find in these days of theme and fun bars) and his missus in the kitchen. The reality is the power of female spending, based on the offices and typing pools, factories and shops of the 'new' North-East. Yet Tyneside has retained a firm grip on a culture derived from the past, ensuring the survival of the old chauvinistic tenets alongside the major social and economic upheavals of the present. Of course, the region's men have a vested interest in preserving and propagating these beliefs – if only to maintain their dominance in the household and their grip on power at a time when 'wor lass' is more likely to be working than 'Geordie'. But how have the region's women adapted so flexibly and readily to change, while the region has retained its distinctively masculine cultural and social mores?

Perhaps the culture of work-division was always more illusory and less rigid than hindsight and history have allowed. It is possible that, unnoticed beneath the noses of the government official and economist, the submerged world of women's work simply rose to the postwar opportunities. Ready-trained in service-work culture, willing and collectively experienced in the ways of work and eminently flexible (and disposable), they have adapted to work because in reality they always did. Certainly, women adapted to the new economic and cultural realities with greater ease than men. Women have always been able to slip between the economic and domestic boundaries, and have long been adept at juggling cultural and social dictates with economic reality. This relatively smooth transition from homeworker to waged worker has not been achieved without cost, however. Maintaining the traditions of the past – the Tyneside woman's reputation for putting home and family first, for upholding the Northern reputations for well-maintained homes, hospitality and table – has added to the double burden of homemaker and worker. It is no coincidence that in a region where women combine past with present, 'dinner on the table' with work, Marks & Spencer's food department reigns supreme.

Nevertheless, Tyneside's women have achieved through work an economic and social revolution without waging cultural war. Sid the Sexist may roam between Tuxedo Royale and Bentley's, but the Fat Slags have beaten him at his own game. Confident, working, and with money to spend and leisure time earned, they have taken elements of that masculine, work-based heritage – the noisy assertion of the right to enjoy life, to spend hard-earned money on hedonistic pursuits and the belief in the importance of their region and its identity – and made them their own. Millie the Maid was in reality always Sharon or Tracey; she just allowed Sid to think he was the kingpin.

CHAPTER SEVEN

Sporting Heroes

HARVEY TAYLOR

THE WORKING-CLASS CULTURE of the North-East has been the subject of constant parody. Stereotyping the region in terms of selected cultural idiosyncrasies is in danger of becoming a popular pastime in itself. Those people whose responsibility it is to promote a new image for the area wage their own battle against what they see as the false and damaging pictures of the region which are projected from the south, but the main source of these stereotypes stems from within the region itself. Grotesque parodies of a local culture, dominated by the whippet and working men's club syndrome, are regularly served up by the producers of Geordie kitsch. The parodies do most certainly point to identifiable aspects of local life, but the true cultural identity is far richer than the packaging suggests.

The new pride in locality which developed in the North-East during the nineteenth century went against the grain of a middle-class rationalism which viewed the oddities and eccentricities of pre-industrial culture as ripe for reform. Yet, far from being smothered, local identity flourished in new and robust forms based on a revived popular culture. In a period of rapid industrial expansion, regional identity developed in tandem with the formation of social class to produce a popular culture which gave expression to the expanding urban working class. A cultural revolution took place in which new sports and pastimes helped to foster a new form of regionalism, a regionalism which in turn was grafted on to an older tradition of provincial identity. The growth and consolidation of this regionalism, in a population containing many immigrants with no native affinity with the area, evolved into a sense of belonging

FIGURE 7.1: 'The importance of sporting pursuits brought forth sporting gladia-
tors.' *The four just men* (1957), Photograph: courtesy of Jimmy Forsyth and West
Newcastle Local Studies Centre (from *Scotswood Road*, Bloodaxe Books, 1986).

which was nourished organically in workplace, pub and in sporting
events.

The importance of sporting pursuits brought forth sporting gla-
diators (see Figure 7.1). The role of the sporting hero in the
North-East was certainly more than simply to be the subject of hero
worship. Backed by the belief that there were many more of this
calibre just waiting to prove their worth, the hero was seen as
typical of the region and representative of its skills and strengths.

This North-East sporting heroism was only part of a broader-
based civic pride. This pride in local achievement, on Tyneside in
particular, was established well before the late Victorian heyday of
municipalism. The redevelopment of Newcastle during the 1830s

in a bold, classical style gave a focus to local self-esteem which in many ways transcended social class. The gregarious, popular dimension to that cultural identity did, however, remain crucial. It often hinged around sporting events, and has been appropriately immortalised in the regional anthem which celebrates the Blaydon Races of 1862. This complex, cross-class, cultural milieu was well established in the North-East, and particularly on Tyneside, long before any really comparable phenomenon can be identified in other areas of the country.

London was the target for a newly evolved North-East patriotism in the mid-nineteenth century. There was always an ironic aspect to this rivalry. Connections of work and trade between the Tyne and the Thames served to fuel the competitive jealousy, producing a continuous sporting rivalry and creating the first regional sporting heroes with whom the working population could identify.

From 'Hadaway Harry' to 'Gazza', the story of the Geordie sporting hero could be said to start and end in Dunston. Henry (Harry) Clasper and Paul Gascoigne, two sporting sons of this industrial suburb of Gateshead, took their skill and reputation to London to achieve an international renown which would boost the esteem of the Geordies. Dunston is a microcosm of the industrial rise and fall of the North-East. Recent dramatic changes in its landscape and function seem to point the way to the future of the region. Along with the adjacent Teams – where Gascoigne was born – the district has experienced rapid redevelopment during the 1980s from industrial wasteland to leisure facility. The old coal-based industries seemed to vanish beneath the massive site of the 1990 'National Garden Festival', a site which is currently being redeveloped into a pleasant, landscaped, residential area. The vast Gateshead Metro Centre shopping and leisure area lies just upriver. This 'modernisation' is mirrored across the river, on the north bank. The careers of Clasper and Gascoigne coincide with the beginning and end of that century and a half of development and redevelopment, from Industrial Revolution to recent radical restructuring which aims uncertainly at a post-industrial future. Along with other sporting heroes, their role has been a significant component of the sustenance of local identity.

It was professional competitive rowing which became the first focal point of sporting pride. As a working river, the Tyne played a central role in the first growth of working-class sports which maintained close relationships with work and the working environment. The proliferation of aquatic contests on the river was not simply the adoption of the existing traditions of gentlemanly amateur rowing by a newly disciplined working class. Instead, rowing was rescued as a popular pastime from the rigid and class-ridden rules and restrictions imposed on working men's sport by elite amateurism. Professional status was the inevitable outcome of the competitors' position as working men. Gamesmanship and tactics became important characteristics of the sporting contest, though, importantly, the real heroes of rowing were seen never to resort to the unfair tactics of the cheat. A sporting ethic was still seen as essential to the contest.

The new professionalism did, however, distinguish working-class rowing from its gentlemanly equivalent. The skill and strength which led to the success of the Tyne rowers, and the huge crowds which they attracted, had firm foundations in the importance of the river as the vital industrial artery of the region. The men of the Tyne were not mimicking the activities of the leisured classes, but were following their own experiences as working watermen in the tradition of keelmen and ferryboatmen.

The huge popularity of rowing matches, and their place as part of a new communal identity, is apparent in contemporary reports.

> Early on the morning of Monday, Newcastle was all stir and animation, and as the day advanced the numerous excursion trains from Sunderland, Consett, Jarrow and other neighbouring towns poured a continuous stream of visitors into the streets, until they became so densely crowded as to be almost impassable. As the hour appointed to the race approached, the river presented a scene, the like of which was confessedly never witnessed by the 'oldest inhabitant'. Every post of vantage, whether on bridge, quay, bank or wall, was occupied by a struggling crowd of eager spectators, which every moment received fresh accessions from the various works and factories.
>
> (*The Sporting Gazette*, 10 September 1864)

The local press not only produced substantial coverage of such events, but also deliberately fostered local pride and fuelled the rivalries with other regions. The report of the *Newcastle Daily Chronicle* was typical. In its hyperbole, there is irony also:

> The question that interests the largest number of people on Tyneside today is not who is to be the new candidate for the representation of

Newcastle or the new President of the American Republic, or whether
Grant will take Richmond or Sherman Atlanta, or whether Louis
Napoleon is seriously ill or only has had a passing bilious attack
consequent upon his late merry making with the King of Spain, but it
is, who will win the Boat Race?

(Newcastle Daily Chronicle, 16 October 1865)

Even more essential to the promotion of local pride were the
balladeers who sang the praises of the new sporting heroes and
described their prowess in a vernacular verse which stylised the
dialect and gave further impetus to the sense of regional
differentness:

> Wor Jack an' Tom, alang wi' me,
> Join'd in the hurry skurry
> That spred alang Newcassel Kee,
> When foaks wi' frantic flurry
> Rush'd here an' there to get a place
> That they might see the greet boat race;
> Alang the Close they madly push'd,
> Byeth foaks an' people sair was crush'd
> An' poor sowls feet that sported corn,
> Wes nice an' clean tho' ruffly shorn,
> When they went te see the race, lads.
>
> (Joe Wilson, *The Greet Boat Race*)

The 'Great Boat Races' which the newspapers and popular songwriters were publicising were the regular rowing matches between
top scullers from Tyne and Thames. Before 1840, any challenge to
the supremacy of 'the supposed invincible Cockneys' was viewed as
a joke. When the Tyne threw down the gauntlet to the Thames, it
stimulated the golden age of Tyneside rowing. The big nineteenth-
century rowing matches became so popular on Tyneside that supporters travelled to London to back their men. *Bell's Life*, the
journal of the sporting 'fancy', remarked on 'the great number of
north countrymen among the spectators at the Thames National
Regatta' and how 'their manly and cheerful "Haud awa' Harry"
reminded us forcefully of days of yore'. Thames-Tyne rivalry was
the mainstay of nineteenth-century professional rowing. What
really mattered was beating London. The men to do it were those
whom the *Newcastle Weekly Chronicle* called 'the robust and expert
watermen of the river.'

Ne men like them had ivor pull'd
Let Tyneside glory shine,
An' lang may champions o' the world
Spring frae the coally Tyne.
(Joe Wilson, *The Greet Boat Race*)

The Cockneys say uz keelmen cheps hez nowther sense nor larnin',
An chef aboot wor tawk, the fuils; but faix, they've got a warnin',
They thowt wor brains wis mixed wi' coals, but noo a change that
     odd is,
Alang wi' coals we send up men that licks the Cockney bodies.
(Ned Corvan, *Wor Tyneside Champions*)

'Had awa' Harry was the first real Geordie sporting hero and, as
such, carried much of the weight of regional expectations. Clasper
worked as a miner, a ship's carpenter, a coke burner and a wherry-
man before rising to rowing fame. It was comprehensive defeat in
1842 and 1844, on both Tyne and Thames, by the famed Robert
Coombes of Vauxhall and his crews, which stimulated Harry to
produce the first serious challenge to the previously unquestioned
primacy of the Thames. In July 1845, the Clasper brothers, Harry,
Robert and William, and uncle Ned Hawks, wrested the 'world
championship' away from London at the Thames Regatta. They
arrived back in Newcastle to a salute from guns and the peal of bells
of All Saints. Clasper's seizure of the laurels from London, and his
many subsequent successes, ensured his position at the centre of
local pride, even if the invincibility legend does not stand up to
scrutiny. The records do not, however, do full justice to the man.
Clasper was born too soon and was past his peak when rowing
reached its height of popularity. The Clasper legend, sustained by
the press and the songwriters – 'The forst brave champein o' wor
Tyneside men' (Joe Wilson) – was due to wider-ranging achievements. Harry's development of training techniques and his technical innovations spread his fame to London and beyond. The
Tyne's reputation extended throughout the rowing world, backed
up by an intense rivalry between local boatbuilders who raced their
own craft. Largely based on Clasper's innovations, Tyne boats
graced regattas throughout the country, as well as being exported
as far afield as Paris, New Orleans, Boston and Sydney. *Bell's Life*
acknowledged in 1861 that 'the Tyne is noted not only for rowers
but also stands first for boat building'.

Tyneside may be proud that she has produced a Stephenson and a Clasper. The former who has revolutionised the whole world in land transit, and the latter for quick water conveyance.

(Newcastle Daily Chronicle, 2 January 1862)

Much of the fame which the rowers and boatbuilders brought to the region can certainly be credited to Harry Clasper. It was, however, two later and more successful scullers who more completely achieved the status of sporting heroes. Robert Chambers and James Renforth carried the name of the Tyne into a much wider arena as rowing developed into an international professional sport. Again, the heroes were men with whom working-class people could identify. Iron puddler 'Honest Bob' Chambers from St Anthony's was a protégé of Clasper who took over the master's mantle and who dominated the world professional sculling championships from 1859 to 1864, beating Australian and Canadian as well as London crews. Chambers's brilliant career was tragically ended by tuberculosis at the age of thirty-six. The fervour of the Tyneside sporting crowd, and the affection that they had for Chambers, was demonstrated by the 60,000 people who 'assembled along the route' of his funeral procession.

Even more impressive was the response which followed the death of Renforth in 1871. An estimated 150,000 turned out to pay their last respects, and a monument, raised by public subscription, was later erected over his grave. Renforth was guaranteed legendary status when he died in dramatic circumstances during a race. Born at Rabbit Banks, Gateshead, in 1842, James Renforth worked as a smith's striker and served as a soldier in the West Indies before becoming a boatman, ferrying workers for the demolition of the old Tyne Bridge in 1866. Early success for the powerfully built Renforth came as a competitive swimmer, but his major fame came in upholding the reputation of his native river in a short-lived but glittering career as a professional sculler. In November 1868, Renforth regained the initiative from the Thames by beating Henry Kelley of Putney for the championship of England. Renforth spread the already considerable renown of the Tyne further afield when in September 1870 he took his crew to Canada to defeat the North American challenge. *The Sporting Gazette* lauded him as 'the finest sculler who ever sat in a boat', and in this he stood in a tradition:

Newcastle had long since come to look on the brawny champion as the rightful heir of the renown which Clasper founded and which Chambers confirmed and extended.

(The Field, September 1871)

Death on the Kennebecassis River at St John, New Brunswick, on 23 August 1871, was the stuff of sporting legend. During the race, Renforth collapsed into the arms of a crewmate and died soon afterwards. At the inquest, there were rumours of dope-taking and poisoning. The knowledge that £30,000 had been wagered on the contest kept the pot boiling. Gambling on such a scale emphasises the fact that nineteenth-century rowers were involved in a serious professional sport, wholly divorced from the upper- and middle-class amateur ethos. The funeral of the man whom the *Daily Telegraph* called a 'simple rough Tyneside waterman' produced unprecedented scenes and was compared in size to that of Cardinal Manning. The scene was vividly described in *The Field*:

> every town and village in the valley of the lower Tyne sent forth its active population to witness the demonstration of sympathy and respect implied in a public funeral ... the line of procession was one dense mass of human beings through which the funeral cortège could hardly cleave its way ... on the route the name of Renforth was a synonym for the honour of the Tyne.
>
> *(The Field*, September 1871)

The achievements of the local rowers continued for some time to be a rallying point for Geordie pride. In their origins, and in their skill and muscularity, Clasper, Chambers and Renforth were heroes who could be seen as ordinary working men acting as role models for the male-dominated working community of their river. The Newcastle Handicap ensured that rowing remained a popular part of local culture right up to the Second World War, yet few people in the area are aware of the important part played by aquatic contests in the development of regional cultural identity. Events on the river during the 'National Garden Festival', and a recently published short biography of Harry Clasper, may help to raise awareness, but, by and large, rowing has been forgotten.

The demise of rowing as the mainstay of local sporting pride was, of course, due to its submergence by the great leviathan of football, but was also closely connected with the changing economy of the river, which reduced the role of the working watermen. Considering 'the extraordinary football traditions and culture of the North-East' (Fishwick, *English Football and Society, 1910-1950*), the 'hotbed of Association football' (John Arlott, 1960) came surprisingly late to the game. Football owed its birth and early development to southern gentlemen amateurs with their Victorian public-school ideas based on the Corinthian principles of fair play and 'muscular Christianity'. The breakaway professionalism of Lancashire, Yorkshire and the Midlands created the modern game. Not until 1883 were the Football Associations of Northumberland and Durham founded, and, although the amateur Northern League (formed in March 1889 at the Three Tuns Hotel in Durham) is the second-oldest football league in the world, North-East participation in the national and professional Football League did not come until the entry of Sunderland in 1890. Once the football phenomenon had taken off, however, it took only a short time to become integrated into the regional male identity (see Figure 7.2).

By the 1890s, local sporting pride and the continuing challenge to the south had shifted from rowing to football. The amateur game showed the way. It was the burgeoning industrial conurbation of Teesside which first seized the initiative from the south, with highly successful teams from Middlesbrough, Stockton and Darlington in

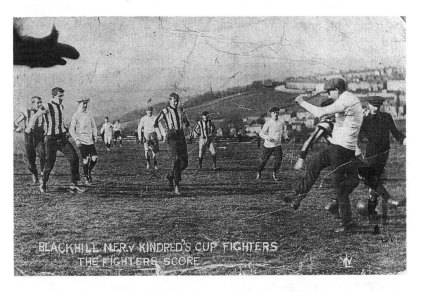

FIGURE 7.2: 'Once the football phenomenon had taken off, however, it took only a short time to become integrated into the regional male identity.' *Blackhill NER v. Kindred's Cup Fighters* (c. 1905), Photograph: Newcastle upon Tyne Libraries and Arts (reproduced by kind permission of Mrs E. Kindred).

the vanguard. Middlesbrough took the FA Amateur Cup from Old Carthusians in 1895, to the consternation of *The Times*, which unsportingly reported that 'no doubt the severe strain of excessive play of late in the cup ties and the long railway journeys affected the game of this fine race of footballers – the CARTHUSIANS'. The Northern League maintained its grip on this prestigious trophy through the turn of the century, and set the trend for a vigorous rivalry between the Northern League and the amateur leagues of London and the Home Counties. The whole of the North-East passionately followed the fortunes of teams which, in the main, represented the mining towns and villages of west Durham but which drew their players from the whole of the region.

North-East amateur football has spawned a number of players who became national names. Brian Clough of Billingham Synthonia, Bob Paisley of Bishop Auckland and Chris Waddle of Tow Law Town are among the most notable products of the Northern League. The strength of amateur football, and its vital part in the life of local communities, has been one of the cultural peculiarities of the North-East. Large crowds, various incentives to top players, and illegal payments – the inquiry into the Crook Town 'tea money' scandal also highlighted just how commonplace and essential such payments had become by the interwar years – gave the local amateur game a professional, competitive edge. The size of the crowds at the big cup matches, which were often played at St James's, Roker or Ayresome, bear witness to the need to establish footballing dominance over a glamorous and overindulged capital. Rivalries between local teams sustained the game, but when the chance to beat London arose, the passions intensified to absorb and unite the whole region. The rivalry was further fermented by the strong belief that the southern sporting establishment consistently and unfairly excluded North-East players from national sides. If Bishop Auckland and Crook Town could dominate the Amateur Cup, why did their players not form the basis of an England amateur side which, up to the end of the 1950s, still carried prestige? A feeling of unfair treatment has been a constant theme, given added impetus by national neglect of top professional players from the region.

The Edwardian era was the first period of professional football success for the North-East. In 1905, the *Newcastle Daily Chronicle* reported 'scenes of wild excitement', reminiscent of the early days of rowing, which accompanied the league and cup successes of Newcastle United:

> Never in the recent history of the town has there been so absorbing an interest displayed over any one event.
>
> *(Newcastle Daily Chronicle*, 15 April 1905)

As with rowing, supporters followed their men to the capital:

> the excursionists were racy of the district, and were well calculated to give Londoners an interesting impression of what workmen on Tyneside are really like.
>
> *(Newcastle Daily Chronicle*, 18 April 1905)

Great crowds assembled at Central Station to welcome home the Newcastle team from five cup finals, or when they brought back the League Championship after victory at Middlesbrough in April 1905.

The Newcastle United sides of that important formative period contained a true local hero whom people could admire as a shining example. Team captain Colin Veitch certainly fitted the bill. He was a man of many parts, both on the field and off. His footballing versatility enabled him to play in four different positions in five cup finals, while he also played a leading role in developing the game with revolutionary new tactics and in pioneering the pre-match tactical talk. As an educated and articulate man of socialist principles, Veitch was the leading light in a nascent players' union, fighting for the rights and working conditions of his fellow professionals. Veitch's lifelong dedication to the cause of Tyneside's working class also led him into a wide range of activities outside football. His multifaceted talents were not an easy model for working men to emulate, but his skilful and robust play, and his tireless work for the people of Newcastle, ensured their lasting admiration. His socialism believed in the need to broaden the horizons of working people through rational and educational forms of leisure, and it is paradoxical that Veitch should have actively pursued such civic principles when he was also the ultimate professional in an increasingly commercialised sport. It was during Veitch's twenty-seven years with Newcastle United that football really became the backbone of North-East identity. In 1901, the 30,000 capacity of St James's Park was invaded by 70,000 Newcastle and Sunderland supporters for the local derby match. The resulting scenes led to the abandonment of the match.

Another aspect of North-East football is also rooted in that early period. Despite the area's national reputation for producing footballers, and the development of a strong junior club structure, there has been an unusually heavy reliance on imported stars in the professional game. During the early years of the century, the North-East was not the football nursery which it later became. The chance to play at a high level in the 'amateur' game with a reasonable level of additional income was always an influence. It was perambulating Scots who dominated football at its highest professional level. Newcastle's championship-winning side of 1926-7 contained seven Scots, while Sunderland were also noted for the number of Scots they recruited, particularly in their successful team of the 1930s. The trend was set at an early stage for local talent to leave the area. The imported stars produced a different type of Geordie sporting hero. Ulsterman Bill McCracken (a contemporary of Veitch and instigator of the notorious offside trap), the great Scot Hughie Gallagher and 'Clown Prince' Len Shackleton are examples of the adopted heroes of the North-East sporting crowd. Significantly, many of the imports chose to remain in the area when their careers in the game ended. Affinity with the local culture has had big pulling power for adopted North-Easterners. Shackleton, the former 'Bevan Boy' from Bradford, was always an honorary Geordie anyway, having worked as fitter's mate to Jackie Milburn at Hazlerigg Colliery after being transferred to Newcastle. Shackleton's adoption as a North-East legend was guaranteed by a six-goal debut for Newcastle and by superlative performances after transferring to Sunderland.

Jackie Milburn recalled that when he was a lad in Ashington, 'boys just disappeared into the ground to work for the rest of their lives as miners'. Milburn was the most famous and best-loved of all the Geordie sporting heroes. He thrilled the Newcastle crowds for fourteen years with his exciting play in football's post-war boom years. This was the period during which Newcastle United attracted a seasonal average home gate of more than 56,000 while playing in the Second Division – a figure which has only once been slightly bettered, by Manchester United playing at the top of the First Division in the 1960s.

'Wor Jackie' possessed all the necessary requisites of the local hero. He was the modest man of the people who came out of the pits to become a genuine legend. Despite representing only one of the region's teams. Milburn had all the attributes of the regional hero of this period, and, most importantly, could have been any North-East working man. His success and popularity were consistent with the belief that there were plenty more where 'Wor Jackie' came from. Milburn always remained the common man, ever ready to chat on the street corner and never changing his accent, unlike many of the area's recent footballing exports, whose response to media attention has been variable grotesque attempts at BBC vowels. Paul Gascoigne has only recently succumbed to this new language. Even when Jackie Milburn left the region in 1957 to finish his playing career and to embark on a brief spell in management, he retained his strong affinity with the North-East. His love for the place and its working-class people was unbreakable:

> 'The only time when I'm really happy is when I come back over the Tyne Bridge and smell the pit heaps.'

It did not matter that it had been a long time since there had been any pit heaps anywhere near the Tyne Bridge. It was the sentiment behind such statements that counted.

Ten years after leaving Newcastle United, Milburn was belatedly awarded a testimonial match. His fears that he might have been virtually forgotten proved unfounded when over 45,000 people turned out on a wet night to pay their respects. During the early stages of Milburn's football career, he had also dabbled in professional athletics, a sporting tradition which the North-East shares with Scotland. Jackie's speed enabled him to compete in the famous Powderhall Handicap off five yards. The prizes, the heavy gambling and a suspicion of shady practices, which are all part of this sport, belong firmly in the area's cultural traditions. From early nineteenth-century competitive 'pedestrianism' for substantial stakes, to the continuing interest in professional sprinting, the North-East has adapted sporting pursuits to its own requirements and assimilated them into its own unique identity. The early competitive tradition, onto which the modern professionalism was grafted, was well represented by the Wilson family of match walkers from Newcastle. George Wilson, who was employed as a messenger to the legal profession, 'would match to go sixty miles with any man' (*Manchester Mercury*, 3 October 1815). He attracted a crowd of 14,000 to Blackheath to witness his attempt to walk 1,000 miles over twenty consecutive days for substantial prize money and wagers.

The importance of the sporting hero was amply demonstrated by the response which followed the death of Jackie Milburn from cancer at the age of sixty-four. On an October Thursday in 1988, an estimated 30,000 people lined the route of the funeral procession to a packed memorial service in St Nicholas's Cathedral. Many tears were shed by both old and young in a show of deep local sentiment. Milburn's nephew Bobby Charlton was impressed by the response:

> 'Tyneside saw him off well. They did him proud, it was a tribute to a great man.'
>
> (*Newcastle Journal*, 14 October 1988)

The following day, Milburn's ashes were scattered at his beloved Gallowgate End of St James's Park. The Jackie Milburn appeal fund was immediately set up to build a memorial to 'Wor Jackie' from public subscriptions. To some people, the whole affair is seen as absurd, and outside the region it is viewed as a Geordie absurdity. What those people fail to understand is the nature of regional sport and the part that it plays in sustaining identity. Memories of Milburn and what he represented mean more to the people of Tyneside than do the eminent Victorians whose memorials punctuate the streets of Newcastle. Standing in front of Lord Armstrong's memorial at Barras Bridge, one young girl was recently heard to ask whether the distant figure who towered above her was 'the first man to land on the moon?'

Football has been the overwhelming obsession of North-East working men throughout the twentieth century. Other sports have produced stars whose success on a world stage has made them heroes. The aggressive athletic style of Steve Cram was always associated with the region as much as it was with his country, and he constantly took advantage of any opportunity to show his loyalty to Sunderland Football Club. Colin Milburn's swashbuckling batsmanship and happy-go-lucky attitude was seen as indicative of how Geordies approached life.

The masculine flavour of the North-East cultural identity, and its obsession with strength and courage, ensured that the region was the busiest fight scene outside the capital in the interwar years. Newcastle had several venues, while many other North-East towns also each had their boxing hall. Again, the theme of challenging London and the rest was essential to a display of pride which helped to sustain a regional mythology. Scores of hungry fighters, finding an escape route from poverty while simultaneously achieving glory in a male culture, made St James's Hall in the centre of Newcastle the notorious 'graveyard of champions'.

Many famous sportsmen have been forced to leave the area to gain fame and fortune. Financial pressures have pushed top footballers into exile ever since the transfer to Arsenal, in 1913, of Jackie ('Jock') Rutherford, Newcastle's flying winger from Percy Main. One of the best players of his era, playing in one of the most successful sides in Football League history, Rutherford was the first of many to go south after a financial dispute with Newcastle United. With football now operating in an international market, the region has found it increasingly difficult to hold on to its talent. The exiles only ever fleetingly fulfilled the role of North-East sporting heroes. The only real exception is Paul Gascoigne, the new superstar of European football. As post-World Cup 'Gazzamania' swept the country, the Geordies were proud that 'Gazza' appeared to remain loyal to the region. He may have been tempted away by London gold, and later by the glamour and riches of the Italian League, but he retains much of his Tyneside identity; the departure can easily be blamed on the unambitious directors of Newcastle United anyway. Now needing more than ever to operate as businesses, the clubs have continued to let the region down. Newcastle United started the 1991-2 season with rising debts of £5,000,000, although Middlesbrough have successfully demonstrated that there can be life after insolvency. 'Gazza' is the Geordie sporting hero for the late twentieth century: rich and famous and not afraid to display the trappings, but managing to portray the image that he is still one of the lads. Just like earlier local heroes, he can be readily identified with. The cheeky and deliberately abrasive style and beefy appearance give the impression of being one of the local lads working up a thirst while playing for his pub or social club team in a Sunday League match. The keenness with which 'Gazza' returns to Dunston's 'Excelsior' working men's club gives him an essential authenticity. He was also apparently unaffected by the fame which followed his World Cup stardom, wanting to be back among his own people and his native place. A big reception at the 'Excelsior' awaited his return:

> ... while a £15m price was put on his head, World Cup hero Paul Gascoigne preferred to fool around with his mates when he arrived on Tyneside.
> (*Newcastle Evening Chronicle*, 10 July 1990)

Gascoigne's connection with the local working men's club is significant in an area where social drinking and its close partner, gambling, have always been closely connected to sporting activity. From the early days, when the rowers received backing from the drink trade – Clasper was even given a pub following his testimonial in 1862 – and the Bacchanalian pursuits which were an integral part of that scene, to the ex-professional footballer publicans of the 1950s and 1960s, this apparently contradictory relationship has long flourished.

Rowing and football both have their origins in an upper- and middle-class ethos, but they were both adapted to suit the needs of a culture with deep roots in the predominantly male workplace and associational life of the region. The working man's belief in the strength and skill of his own type has been given popular expression in a sporting hero with whom he can identify. This athletic aspect of the culture evolved separately from the sporting guidelines devised by the Victorian middle class. It adopted a professional, highly competitive and distinctly regional flavour, while also integrating characteristics which gave a closer cultural affinity with dubious aristocratic traditions of leisure: drink, conviviality and money. It has, however, been a culture made by the people from the bottom up, producing an ethos which grew out of the workplace and pub, the club and the neighbourhood. The creation of a particular type of sporting hero, representing male skills and male interests, has been consistent with the region's labour tradition (see Figure 7.3). In formal representations, at least, women's work and women's status have always been marginalised.

From keel and ferryboat rowers to the current structure of amateur and junior football, participation has been central. In recent years, the 'Great North Run' has been the most obvious manifestation of that need to participate and to identify with the top performers. Brendan Foster's 'Great North Run' may have evolved as part of a national vogue for the 'fun run', conceived as a means of encouraging more people to exercise, but its success as a major event has in no small measure been due to its consistency with the role of sport in North-East cultural tradition. It needs to be seen to be big enough and brash enough to cock a snook at the highly publicised London Marathon, while also enjoying the status of premier event of its kind in the country. Participation in the Run absorbs a large proportion of the whole community, including the enthusiastic crowds who line the route to offer refreshment and encouragement to the runners. There is a longer tradition of athletic participation represented by the New Year's Day Morpeth to Newcastle Road Race, which is a generally more serious athletic event, but which similarly attracts enthusiastic crowds who spill out of the pubs and clubs to cheer the runners. There is a firm base for these road races in the thriving athletic clubs of the region. In a democratic sport such as this, there is the chance for anyone to run winter cross-country against Steve Cram, or to compete in a road race against Mike McLeod.

It has been this 'Great North Run' and the underlying athletic club structure which have presented the first real challenge to male dominance in regional sport. Hundreds of women participate in the 'Great North Run', the athletic clubs have a considerable female membership, and it is now common for the women to train with the men. There may be a long way to go before male dominance is overturned, but the democracy of running has produced the first genuine chink in the work-determined culture. The idea of the

FIGURE 7.3:   'The creation of a particular type of sporting hero, representing male skills and male interests, has been consistent with the region's labour traditions.' *Riveters on board ship* (1920s), Photograph: South Tyneside Libraries.

Geordie sporting heroine is no longer inconceivable, represented, for example, by Jill Hunter, a working woman, living in the North-East, who can challenge the rest of the world.

The increase in female participation in North-East sport in the last quarter of the century is the inevitable corollary of universal trends, but it is surprising just how tenacious the old culture has been. In a post-industrial world in which the structure of the old industrial regional economy has been seriously eroded, and the nature of work and the workplace radically altered, there is abundant evidence of the continued strength of a masculine, working-class, regional identity. The 'pit villages' may no longer have any pits, and the larger workplaces have either been drastically rationalised or no longer exist as focal points, but the old recreational pursuits still survive, and, in many instances, prosper. The whippet races at the 'Welfare' or the 'Institute' are still a feature of Sunday mornings; leeks and leek shows are both bigger and better than during the industrial heyday; and any threat to the pigeon crees on the allotments comes not from cultural demise but from the property developer and from the financial pressures on local councils. As a world game, football has irrevocably changed, and the state of the region's big three professional clubs continues to be an embarrassment, but it is still perceived as our game and remains the main obsession.

What this survival really underlines is the resilience of a cultural heritage. The post-industrial leisure- and services-orientated economy may have imposed new influences and attractions, with enterprise capitalism demanding a highly commercialised leisure industry, but that is not an entirely new phenomenon. There has been a strong commercial dimension in North-East recreational culture going back at least into the nineteenth century. *Rational* recreation has, by and large, been a failure. Popular culture rose to the fore to give the region a unique aspect to its identity, and it continues to serve as a unifying force which can be projected into the future. The old North-East cultural identity was strongly influenced by male work. Its modern equivalent stems from a response to the virtual destruction of that work-base. Against increasing pressures for national uniformity, the regional unifying force of an ingrained popular culture continues to demand autonomy and stubbornly resists assimilation.

CHAPTER EIGHT

Black Geordies

BARRY CARR

THE PARK ON THE LAWE TOP at South Shields may not be the finest playing surface in the world for football, but the view, especially for a Geordie, would be hard to beat. One touchline drops dramatically to the point where the River Tyne meets the North Sea, and any inactive winger can look down on a composition of images ingrained in the memory of every Tynesider: the river itself, subject of a thousand songs and poems that reflect the fortunes of its people; the Fish Quay over the water at North Shields; skeletal Tynemouth Priory; the fairground at South Shields clinging to the beach; granite piers stretching out to sea; and Admiral Collingwood perched on his column, contemplating for eternity Nelson's message at Trafalgar. A Geordie panorama.

Not that the players on this perfect summer's evening had time to appreciate the view. The World Cup in Italy had fired their enthusiasm and made the match a constantly flowing contest. The startling variety of the players' strips even made the game appear to be a microcosm of that event, as Dutch, German, Brazilian and English shirts merged into one vivid international confusion. The colour of the players' skins reinforced the Italian image, as black, brown and white boys appeared to make up the two sides in equally random numbers.

The majority of the dark-skinned boys were sons of Bangladeshi workers in the town's numerous 'Indian' restaurants. They were divided between the two sides, but within their own ranks had formed a further division that saw those wearing Newcastle football shirts opposing those in Sunderland's colours. The two groups had made their allegiances within a difference at the heart of Geordie culture. Their commitment to one or other of the clubs was an intriguing example of regional identification. To see it displayed in such an evocative setting conjured up a vision of social cohesion that a myriad of reports, statistics and inquiries could never communicate: Black Geordies.

That such a vision should materialise in South Shields might not appear surprising to those who are aware of the town's reputation in the field of race relations. David Bean informed *Guardian* readers on 1 March 1962 that 'Shields is a study in integration; a place where colour prejudice died years ago'. Many journalists subsequently delivered judgements similar to Bean's. This universal accord had given South Shields a unique standing in the history of race relations in this country.

The basis for this standing has always been the perceived racial harmony between the Arab and white inhabitants of the town. The Arab community was originally formed by seamen from Yemen who settled in South Shields during the 1890s. While other Muslim seamen from Africa and the Indian subcontinent also have a long history in the town, the Yemenis have always been in the forefront and, in the public eye, represent the 'black' presence in Shields. Although other communities of seamen settled in this country at the same time, including large Yemeni settlements in Cardiff and Liverpool, it is only South Shields that has achieved such a reputation for racial harmony. This suggests a regional dimension: Black Geordies are 'Geordies' first.

This notion however, is dependent on the validity of the judgements made by Bean and his fellow commentators on South Shields, and on the assumption that the town is representative of the North-East. When Bean wrote his article, the Arab community in Shields was the only substantial group of black people in the region. Since then, substantial Bangladeshi communities have formed in Newcastle and Sunderland. It is necessary to compare the experiences of these communities with that of South Shields before a definitive judgement can be made on the North-East as a whole. Even more pertinent, perhaps, is the need first to examine in detail the claims made on behalf of Shields. Is it really 'The Town Where Colour Doesn't Count'?

'South Shields has a bad name all over the world among the coloured people.' This was the view of a Pan-African Federation official in 1950. It suggests that, certainly at this time, racial harmony was not yet a predominant feature of the town. The only serious research on the town's Arab community, S. F. Collins's *Coloured Minorities in Britain*, carried out in the same period, supports this impression. Collins makes no reference, in any part of his work, to the town having a good reputation for race relations. The key to understanding how this good reputation was bestowed ten years later lies in a history of the Arab community itself and on the climate of race relations in Britain at the time of the bestowal.

Media interest in Shields was prompted by the Notting Hill Riots of 1958. These were the first public outbreak of racial conflict in postwar Britain. To many observers, they marked the beginning of 'the colour problem'. It led Philip Rawstrone in the *Shields Gazette* on 25 February 1959 to see South Shields as an answer to that problem.

Rawstrone saw the absence of physical conflict in the town between blacks and whites as a lesson to the racial trouble spots of Britain. 'In no other part of the country has the problem been handled so well,' he claimed. To his credit, Rawstrone did attempt to explain that 'It has taken time to achieve this. South Shields has had its disturbing moments, its racial mobs.' Unfortunately, the cause and result of these disturbances were not expanded on. Rawstrone's only aim was to reassure the rest of Britain that Shields's surface calm proved that displays of racial conflict elsewhere were not inevitable. Negative factors, for admirable reasons no doubt, were not allowed to impinge on his promotion of Shields as a beacon of hope.

But Rawstrone found it difficult to explain the phenomenon. He suggested, without any conviction, that 'Perhaps ... the innate friendliness of the Geordie', or the 'patience which men learn in the East', were the causes. The local government officials, politicians and police chiefs he quoted were equally vague in their reasons. The main justification was provided by the verbal testimony of the Arab community: 'No colour bar. Not even a colour problem here.'

Visitors like Bean who followed in Rawstrone's footsteps accepted his central premise and gave even less attention to the historical perspective. Shields was portrayed as never having experienced racial tension or conflict of any substance. The visits of these journalists also coincided with examples of the racial violence elsewhere which had first attracted Rawstrone. Recent instances of controversy involving Islam, such as the Rushdie Affair and the

Gulf War, have also prompted journalistic visits. The temptation to use Shields as oil on troubled waters once again proved irresistible.

The Arab community was happy to play its part in these exercises. It knew the danger of publicly opposing the role allocated to it by the host society from the experience of Ali Said, the first Yemeni to settle in the town. Ali Said stood up against racial prejudice, defended the rights of the Arab community, refused to accept manipulation and bullying, and was deported for his troubles. The message was not lost on the Arabs. Said's sojourn in the town covered the community's formative years; his departure signalled the shape it finally took.

The process that brought Ali Said and his fellow Yemenis to a corner of North-East England in the 1890s was a haphazard one. They had left their own country on the Arabian peninsula to seek work on the British ships that passed through the colony of Aden. This journey brought them to Britain, and gradually led some individuals, for various reasons, to establish roots in particular ports. In Ali Said's case, this happened to be Shields.

Ali was a ship's fireman, as all the Yemenis were. The job consisted of feeding coal into the ship's boilers – a dirty and exhausting task carried out in the suffocating heat and noise of the stokehold. Havelock Wilson, the seamen's union leader, estimated that one in every two hundred firemen who started a trip returned certifiably insane. The job required no skill or command of the English language though, and this suited the Yemenis. Most were originally farm workers from the north of Yemen who had no industrial skills nor the ability to speak English.

The nature of their labour was a vital factor in the development of the Arab community. While they were working, they had no contact with Shields or its people. Even aboard ship, firemen were a group apart, and, as they were traditionally made up of one national or racial class, the Yemenis had little need for contact with British crewmates. When they were ashore, the Merchant Shipping Acts insisted that all seamen without private residences had to live in a Licensed Seamen's Boarding House. This further insulated the Yemenis from the normal flow of life in Shields.

Not that the host society showed much enthusiasm for mixing. Francie Nichol ran a boarding house in Shields at the turn of the century. When it came to lodgers, she had her standards:

We didn't have many coloured fellers in because of the trouble ye always got, but at one time I had these coal black darkies for a few days. They seemed quiet and well mannered enough. They had come off a ship and wanted somewhere to stay. Nobody else would take them so I said I would as long as it was only for a few days.

(Quoted in Joe Robinson,
The Life and Times of Francie Nichol of South Shields 1975)

The Yemenis had trouble finding accommodation. Cafes and other public places refused them entry. The hostility they encountered, together with the dictates of their religion that the host society would not and could not cater for, forced the Yemenis to rely upon themselves. Ali Said opened the first Arab Seamen's Boarding House in August 1909. Here the men could carry on their cultural and religious life without recourse to the outside world.

Said's house was in the Holborn district of the town, by the riverside. Before 1914, there were only a few dozen Yemenis in South Shields and, restricted to the Holborn area, they made little impression on the town. The advent of the First World War dramatically changed the situation.

The horrific casualties of the war led to manpower shortages in the Merchant Navy. The government and shipowners actively encouraged Yemenis into this country to fill the vacancies. The Arab community in Shields increased to around 3,000 by the end of the war. Seven hundred Arab firemen sailing from Shields lost their lives during the conflict. Not that this sacrifice was recorded on the War Memorials and Rolls of Honour that sprouted up in practically every street. As a memory, the sacrifice was confined to the Arab community. If the town's Arabs thought their service would be subsequently recognised, they were quickly disillusioned. The end of the war saw the start of a concerted campaign of racial violence and discrimination aimed at driving every Arab out of the town.

'You black bastards, this ship is not for you', were the words of John Fye, a seamen's union official who in 1919 summed up the attitude of Shields to its Arab population. By substituting the word 'town' for 'ship', Fye's comment might have summarised the many letters appearing in the *Shields Gazette* for February and March 1919 asking for the Arabs to be deported. In the opinion of the white community, the Arabs were transient, migrant workers who should move on when their services were no longer required. The shipping slump after the war meant that discharged soldiers and sailors returning to Shields found no work waiting for them. They were not prepared to see the Arabs take what little there was.

Fye did not hide behind a nom de plume like the letter-writers. He addressed his remarks directly to a Yemeni waiting on the Mill Dam, a cobbled square by the riverside where ships' crews were hired. Sixty seconds later, as he lay on the cobbles with a broken arm, his face cut and a Yemeni sitting on his chest aiming a knife at his throat, Fye had learnt two things: one, the advantage of noms de plume and two, the fact that these particular 'black bastards' were not going anywhere without a fight.

The result of Fye's outburst was 'Turbulent scenes the likes of which had never before been seen in South Shields', as the *Gazette* reported under the headline 'Arab Riot'. In February 1919, hundreds of white seamen and Arabs fought on the Mill Dam. Revolvers, knives, sticks and bottles were used in a battle that the police could not quell. A detachment from the Durham Light Infantry, together with 'bluejackets' from Royal Navy ships moored in the Tyne, were needed to restore order. Eight Arabs were sent to prison for their part in the riot; Fye was bound over for using language likely to cause a breach of the peace.

The riot may have been sparked off by a dispute over jobs, but it was only symptomatic of the racial violence against the Arabs during the previous months. In January, the first Arab boarding house that attempted to open outside the confines of Holborn was wrecked and looted by a mob of white residents numbering over 400. J. Muir Smith, a local solicitor, testified that 'The life of these Arab firemen is becoming intolerable ... an Arab is now afraid to walk the streets'.

The onslaught continued throughout the 1920s. Unprovoked assaults against Yemenis standing at their own front doors were commonplace. A journey outside Holborn, especially to the Market Place, almost guaranteed a fight. Physical violence was accompanied by a steady stream of invective in the *Gazette*. 'Clinker' informed readers that the Arabs had been 'hopeless in action' during the war, 'terrified and a hinderance'. 'M.C.H.', 'Burgoo' and many others heaped abuse on them, demanding that they be deported to their 'native land so that they can eat rice, sell oranges, and do the other things that the Good Lord put them on earth for'.

The Arabs had all been single men when they came to Shields. Their marriages to local women provoked rather than appeased their detractors. 'C. Brown' urged that force be used to remove the Arabs and 'their outcast children and shameless wives ... they are a plague'. 'Holborn Resident' complained that Arabs were paying inflated rents for houses and shops, thereby driving white residents out of the district. 'H.B.' declared that 'no mixed breed child will ever be as good as children born of white parents', and that they should all be sent back to Aden.

If the Arabs were working, they were accused of depriving white men of jobs; if they were not, then they were lazy spongers who were a financial drain on the town's ratepayers. In fact, few Arabs qualified for dole, or even applied for it if they did. The boarding-house keepers provided subsidies when their boarders were unemployed and were repaid when the men found work. The Arabs, despite being members of the seamen's union, were continually represented as cheap labour. Regular denials made little impression on the critics, and the myths became accepted fact.

Local politicans were prominent in their racism. Councillor Cheeseman informed a 1929 council meeting that, after closely studying the Arabs' languages, customs and general conditions, he could honestly say 'that it is not fit for them to live among white people'. The *Shields Gazette* for 7 February 1929 went on to report Councillor Linney's discovery that Arabs had 'peculiar traits of character and life', that he did not regard them as 'desirable neighbours', and that 'they should not be encouraged'.

The council adopted a deliberate policy – outside its legal powers – of refusing Arabs licences for boarding houses in an attempt to prevent the growth of the community. Abdul Hamid fell foul of this policy in 1929 when his application was refused amid a welter of racial abuse. Hamid appealed to the council that their refusal put his wife and three sons in a serious position, but to no avail. (Fourteen years later, the *Shields Gazette* would carry a picture of Sgt Hasan Joseph Hamid, the eldest of those three sons and a WO/AG in the RAF, reporting that he had been shot down over Germany.)

Individual Arabs met the physical attacks with courage. Renowned in the Middle East for their proud and combative natures, the Yemenis confronted violence head-on. Regarding fistfights as vulgar, they traditionally settled disputes with knives, one peculiar trait which eventually earned them a degree of wary respect.

Ali Said took a prominent position in answering the attacks from councillors and the *Gazette*'s correspondents. Displaying a sardonic style that revealed an impressive command of the English language, Said not only defended his community but also launched pre-emptive attacks of his own. He promised that the Arabs in Shields would return home if all the Englishmen working in Aden did the same. He declared that 'We, although coloured, have helped make the Empire what it is'. He advised impoverished white seamen to follow the Arab example by not making public houses 'going concerns'. He mocked his adversaries by explaining that he was 'only trying to make the likes of "WH" see how dense they were'. Said always gave his full name and address. His public stand earned him few friends outside Holborn.

Events in 1930 brought Ali Said's role as champion of the Arab cause to a wider audience than South Shields. The National Union of Seamen, a corrupt body in the pocket of the shipowners, was facing a serious challenge from the newly formed Minority Movement. The Movement was a Communist-backed attempt to supplant the established trade unions and was enjoying its greatest success among seamen. Fearing that a national strike was imminent, the NUS introduced a rota system of employment for its 'coloured' members that effectively divided the union into two groups. The NUS hoped that, if a strike materialised, the black seamen, impoverished by the restricted work opportunities of the rota system, could be used as strike-breakers. Ali Said immediately realised the implications of the rota. He publicly informed the union leadership that 'coloured seamen are not going to accept the rota system. They will support the white seamen, they will not be used against them.' Said became the national leader of Arab opposition to the rota, and South Shields became the focus of national opposition. M. Ferguson, a leading Communist Party official, thundered that 'We have to make South Shields the storm centre of the fight' (see Figure 8.1). The scheme was introduced on 1 August 1930, and the Arabs solidly refused to sign on. Minority Movement leaders called on white seamen to join the Arabs by refusing to sail as a protest against their own grievances. Support for what was now a strike against the union grew among white

FIGURE 8.1: '"We have to make South Shields the storm centre of the fight."' *Seamen's meeting at Mill Dam* (1930), Photograph: South Tyneside Libraries.

seamen as the Arabs held fast. The government, union and ship-owners were mortified by the possible consequences of a successful strike.

Ali Said's stand came to an end on 2 August. That day saw another battle on the Mill Dam, a battle that broke the Arab opposition to the rota, crushed the national strike and emasculated the Minority Movement. It was a very good day for certain parties and a disastrous day for the Arab community that they never forgot.

The conflict was started by an insult remarkably similar to the one that had started the 1919 riot. 'Come on you black bastards, try to stop me signing on' was directed at Yemeni seamen by a white man named Hamilton. Hamilton was a blackleg who had taken a place on a ship vacated by Arabs who had refused to sign the rota. Minority Movement officials claimed Hamilton was an *agent provocateur*. If so, he was an extremely successful one. The Yemenis attacked Hamilton and were immediately baton-charged by the fifty police officers positioned at the Mill Dam.

Unlike the 1919 riot, the actual fighting was not between white and Arab seamen. The white seamen present made no attempt to help Hamilton or the police. The police directed their charge solely at the Arabs. The resulting clash was a desperately violent affair as the Mill Dam became 'a seething mass of fighting Arabs and police'. Police batons cracked open Arab heads. Knives, razors and revolvers were used by the Arabs. A knife punctured the lung of PC Harry Gash, a near-fatal wound, and Constables Addison and Darling were stabbed also. Eventually, the Arabs were driven back into Holborn.

Ali Said did not take part in the fighting. The only police evidence against him was that he had talked to the Arabs before the fight. He was heard to shout 'Waqaf. Waqaf' (Stop), as the Arabs attacked Hamilton. It could not be determined in court whether he was encouraging or restraining the men. The outrageously biased Judge Roche expressed no doubts in his address to the jury at the trial: 'They came prepared and Ali Said was the only agent who could tell them ... I am quite satisfied that he was at the bottom of this.' Ali Said was convicted of incitement to riot. He was one of fifteen Arabs jailed and subsequently deported for their parts in the riot. The local leaders of the Minority Movement were also jailed on the same charge as Said.

The punishment handed out to Ali Said made a deep impression on the Arab community, particularly the leaders, who now fully appreciated the power of the host society and the fate that awaited those whom it considered to be troublemakers.

This message was reinforced later in 1930. The Arabs had signed the rota, but, with the threat of a strike removed, the NUS was able to exact revenge by severely restricting their employment opportunities. The Arab boarding-house keepers in Shields subsidised their men until they bankrupted themselves. The Public Assistance Committee refused the keepers outdoor relief for the men. As a protest, the keepers sent their boarders to the Poor House for institutional relief. Thirty-eight Arabs who spent one night in the Poor House were deported as destitute aliens. This affair, coming so soon after the riot deportations, crushed the spirit of the Arab community.

Their plight was revealed in an interview which Hassan Mohamed gave to the *Newcastle Evening Chronicle*. Poignantly, the article was published on Christmas Eve 1931.

> I do not think the public know the extent to which the Arabs are suffering. Many have had to pawn clothing and other personal belongings to buy food. There are scores of Arabs in Holborn who are living on one meal a day. We do not grumble, everything comes from God and the men are suffering quietly; they only want a chance to earn a living and believe that they only have the British flag behind them.

It was from this nadir in the Arab community's fortunes that the process began which resulted in the apparent racial harmony that so intrigued visitors to the town thirty years later. Whatever Shields has achieved in the field of race relations, and it is considerable, must always be viewed in the light of the racial prejudice that existed before (see Figure 8.2). The true message, and hope, that South Shields can give to the rest of Britain is that racial tolerance is possible after such a horrific beginning.

Hassan Mohamed's confession that the Arabs had nothing but the British flag behind them was not an admission of defeat, more the beginning of a pragmatic campaign based on the realisation that cooperation, not confrontation, was the only course open after the events of 1930. Hassan Mohamed was cleverly appealing to that sense of fair play and decency associated with the British flag; an association which the state had promulgated as justification for the Empire's expansion. Mohamed was not asking that the Arabs should be allowed to be British, or stating that they would behave like the British, whatever that might be, only that his community should be granted one of the rights that the flag was said to guarantee.

That the process towards attaining these rights had begun after 1930 may not have been immediately obvious to Hassan Mohamed and his community. In 1933, the Public Assistance Officer was still maintaining that 'these men are a serious menace'. Alderman Dunlop, worried by the 1934 Slum Clearance project, insisted that 'these men must be kept in Holborn at all costs'. The editor of *The Shieldsman* declared in 1935 that 'Since it seems impossible to send these people home, the next best thing is to segregrate them'. That

FIGURE 8.2: 'Whatever Shields has achieved in the field of race relations, and it is considerable, must always be viewed in the light of the racial prejudice that existed before.' *Two arrests, Mill Dam riot* (1930), Photograph: South Tyneside Libraries.

is exactly what the council did. A small council estate was built in Laygate, adjacent to Holborn, and let exclusively to the Arab community.

Despite these examples of continued prejudice, criticism of the Arabs diminished during the 1930s. So did its intensity. The physical assaults also gradually diminished until they quietly vanished during the war. No specific time, policy or action can be identified as marking the start of the process.

The process evolved without laws or regulations, committees or reports. It was not imposed or legislated. It was worked out between the Arabs and their white, working-class neighbours in the Laygate district who came to accept their new neighbours in a thousand individual, idiosyncratic encounters and accommodations. The Arabs did not become loved overnight; gradual toleration is a better description, and toleration on both sides at that.

The failure of racism to dominate relationships in South Shields is a subject that demands a level of investigation more than a chapter can bear. Some have argued that it was easier for the Arabs to relate to a regional identity than a national one. The Englishness of the North-East has long been ambivalent. For Shields Arabs and whites alike, Englishness – or what has passed as Englishness – was high up and far away. English national identity was invested in the south. Shields and the North-East were different and apart. The closeness of a strong regional identity must have affected the Arabs.

It could follow on from this argument that the importance of the regional dialect in identifying the 'Geordie' must have helped the process. 'Geordie' is a dialect as well as a person. Once the children of the Arab community opened their mouths to speak, they made their bid for regional identity. Even the diverse levels of competence their fathers reached in spoken English contained the accent and choice of words peculiar to 'Geordie'.

There may also have been an unconscious reaction from many white inhabitants to the actual implementation in 1930 of the racist cant and theories displayed during the 1920s. When the practical results of this prejudice became apparent, many people must have realised that the whole ethos of Tyneside working-class culture was anathema to the bullying on which racism is built. Certainly, many Shields inhabitants must have felt a sense of shame on reading the *Gazette*'s description on 31 January 1931 of the deportation of the 'destitute aliens':

> The men who went last night had not committed any crime ... Just before 9.30 ... the 38 men came from the cells at the Central police station past a double line of police officers into the two police patrol vans waiting ... They were driven to the goods entrance at the railway station and lined up at the end of the platform ... They were very quiet. They ranged from mere boys to venerable men, typically Mohammedan. Many of them held in their hands small parcels containing their supper. This is Ramadan ... and the men had fasted all day ... at 9.50 the train steamed out of the station and bore the Arabs from South Shields.

This abject defeat impressed itself on the town's collective mentality. The Arabs were no longer a threat, an object of fear. They were now the underdogs – a position with which the majority of Tynesiders could identify.

Supporters of the Arabs now began to take a visible public stand. Councillor Gompertz, himself descended from a Jewish family who fled pogroms in Eastern Europe, championed their cause in the council chamber along with Councillor Edmund Hill, a Conservative who also became business adviser to the Arabs in their plan to build a mosque. Victor Grunhut, a wealthy solicitor born in Germany, helped the Arabs both legally and financially. The *Gazette* and *Shieldsman*, which were still the main typifiers of the Arab community to the majority of whites, began to print sympathetic articles about the Arabs and their lifestyle. Stories connected with the community began to appear with the headline 'Shields Arabs ...'; for many years it had just been 'Arabs ...'. In a period before the advent of legislation prohibiting the publication of racially offensive material, the racist letters which had for many years been a feature of the *Gazette* disappeared.

The role of the Arab community in this genesis was not a passive one. Once the Arabs were allowed to follow their chosen lifestyle without hindrance, a reputation for hard work, honesty, generosity and affability slowly impressed itself on the host society. Culturally, the community did not integrate. They maintained their cultural and religious life within the Laygate area. The Arabs had to make some concessions, but they did so pragmatically, not subserviently.

Mohsin Yehia, Yemeni-born, avers that 'life is hard everywhere'. Mohsin, a retired seaman, has been in South Shields since 1957, and has come to a happy accommodation with the town. While Mohsin Yehia still retains his Yemeni citizenship, he is extremely proud of his standing and good reputation in South Shields. He has warned his sons of the consequences if the police ever have to call at his door. But Mohsin Yehia has also told them that if they ever come up against racism, 'Not the silly kids' stuff, name-calling, but blatant racism,' then they must fight it, 'and I'll pay your fine, I'll stand up in court for you'.

Fortunately, Mohsin Yehia's sons have never had to appear in court. Instead, the behaviour and experiences of the Anglo-Arab population have been a major factor in creating the relaxed racial atmosphere of the town. Ignored by the visiting media in their search for clues to the town's racial harmony, those children of the mixed marriages who so worried the early racists are today 'Black Geordies'.

Unquestionably Shields folk, practically all the Anglo-Arabs have joined the Geordie version of national identity. Still retaining their links with the Arab community, they have dispersed throughout the town, following a wide variety of jobs. Their racial and ethnic origin, and loyalty, have had to bargain with the fact that they are Geordies too.

The absence of racial prejudice by the local white population towards the Arabs and Anglo-Arabs is a unique phenomenon. Not that Shields is a town without racists. The descendants of 'Burgoo' and 'Clinker' still remain. There is even an offshoot of the National Front for the lost and the lonely to join if they wish. What is striking is that the prejudice of these unfortunates is always directed externally. To them, the 'colour problem' seems to be something that exists elsewhere, not in South Shields. Their racist rhetoric, anger and forecasts always concern other areas of the country. When asked why their dire prophecies have not materialised in their own town when it has such a large coloured population, they cannot reply. They have never taken it into account. They have missed the evidence in front of them.

Similarly, the lack of the racial assaults that are common in other parts of Britain is testimony to the lack of local prejudice. Even on Tyneside, South Shields has a reputation for violence, but racial assaults are unknown.

The absence of local prejudice can be gauged by the testimony of black inhabitants. The experience of individuals is invariably subjective, but from hundreds of conversations a consensus can be found.

Abdullah Hasan, the Anglo-Arab owner of a shop in Laygate, was born in South Shields. His recollection that he never encountered racial prejudice until he left the town is typical. Conversations with Arabs and Anglo-Arabs during the Gulf War revealed that they were pleased to be in South Shields, not elsewhere in Britain.

This regional dimension is also recognised by the town's Bangladeshi community, who, for those not convinced by anecdotal evidence, express their conviction with their feet. Abu Sufian, a leading member of that community, testifies that many families have deliberately moved to South Shields from Bangladeshi communities elsewhere in Britain. They are not attracted for economic reasons (the restaurant business which is the mainstay of the community is in deep recession), but for social reasons.

The Bangladeshis, although separated physically and culturally from the Arabs, have benefited from the atmosphere of racial tolerance forged in the town by the Arabs. Abu Sufian believes that parents are drawn by the prospect of raising their children in an atmosphere relatively free from racial tension and harassment.

South Shields is not, of course, the North-East. The Bangladeshi community in Newcastle and Sunderland suffers from the physical attacks and abuse that once plagued Shields. Nevertheless, there is still reason to believe that the level of racial harassment in the North-East is not as intense as that elsewhere. Zulficar Ahmed, a Bangladeshi living in Gateshead, is clear that families are attracted to the region by its perceived reputation for community spirit and collectivism, qualities they can identify with and have not found in more Thatcherite areas of the country. Like the mutual qualities upon which the whites of Shields and their Arab neighbours built a relationship, there is the possibility that the newcomers will reinforce rather than alter that old regional identity.

Because of cultural and social differences, it would be foolish to expect the South Shields Bangladeshis to come to exactly the same accommodation as the Arabs. Similarly, on a national scale, it is not possible to cite South Shields as a definite model for the future of race relations in this country. Even so, the town's experience raises some interesting possibilities. The shape this future takes in each place will depend on the regional identity of those places. South Shields's history does suggest that the North-East identity has the character and flexibility to make this future a decent one.

But for how long can the Geordies survive? The prolonged social strains caused by the economic decline of the past thirty years must ultimately have some weakening effect on the identity of the North-East. Perhaps the confidence that fosters racial tolerance may be one of the casualties? It was gratifying to see that the riots of September 1991 did not contain a racial element, but, as the traditions and values of the area are eroded, racism may become a more dominant force that will come to exclude the new immigrants and their children from the mainstream of a stunted new 'Geordieism'.

It is to be hoped that the spirit of South Shields will be the one that prevails. It would be a tragedy if the North-East were to let economics disfigure what is best in its identity. The riches of Tyneside have never been measured purely by money. Whoever heard of a rich pitman or shipwright? It was the character of its people which gave the North-East its real value. If we can maintain our togetherness and remember where we came from, then the future for the Black Geordies, for all Geordies, can be a good one. Let us hope so. There were some very good players in those black and white shirts on the Lawe Top.

CHAPTER NINE

Living the Past Differently
Historical Memory in the North-East

BILL WILLIAMSON

IT WAS 1974. The miners were on strike and their action threatened seriously the pay norms and incomes policy of the Conservative government of Edward Heath. Upstairs on the bus to Throckley from Newcastle, going along the Scotswood Road (of 'Blaydon Races' fame; see Figure 9.1), there were two boys in front of me. One said to the other: 'What you watching on the telly the neet?' 'That thing aboot Churchill and the war', his friend replied. 'Me dad won't let us watch that', said the first boy. 'He says Churchill sent the troops against the miners.' He spoke in a matter-of-fact way without complaint or criticism. Without being aware of it, both these boys were sharing something of the popular memory of miners from the Tyne valley. Their exchange reveals unambiguously the ways in which, through quite ordinary encounters, the elements of a community's sense of its past are reproduced from one generation to the next.

Throckley pit closed in 1955, a good ten years before these boys were born. But there is not a family in the district without roots in the pits and without memories stretching back to 1926 and 1921 and even further. As the boys grew up, these fragments will have been connected. They will have learned more of how their parents and grandparents lived their lives, and they will have acquired the appropriate frameworks of interpretation to make sense of it all.

Memories such as these are a benchmark against which to measure the present and a powerful bond among those who share them; they are markers of a communal identity which binds

FIGURE 9.1: '... going along the Scotswood Road ...' *Outside the Royal Oak, Scotswood Road* (1957), Photograph: courtesy of Jimmy Forsyth and West Newcastle Local Studies Centre (from *Scotswood Road*, Bloodaxe Books, 1986).

families and communities together. Only strangers are unaware of them, and changes in the images and feelings which are part of them mark the slowly altering boundaries of communities and their collective sense of belonging.

The community is, of course, an imagined one. It is us; us Geordies – people from Newcastle, the Tyne Valley, Northumberland, even those from Wearside, South Tyneside and Durham. It is us as we see and are seen, with our hearts of gold, ready humour, our friendliness and flat northern vowels. The stories we know are from our past, not the past of those to the north into Scotland or south beyond the Tees or west of the Pennines, but of those who belong to 'Geordieland'. The recalled elements of that past evoke a story of struggle and exploitation, a tale of victories, and defeats, of courage and of great human dignity in the face of hardship. Being imagined does not make the past and the stories which go with it any less real. But observers must take care to note the occasions when the reality of it matters and when it does not. They must learn to distinguish the occasions when it suits people in the North-East to assume their regional identities, to take their history seriously, and when it does not. For how the past is used and imagined is something shaped by the circumstances of the present; it is something, therefore, which changes through time.

The most potent images of the region's past are those from the mining districts, but the important ones are by no means confined to the coal industry. The boys who caught my attention were from a mining district. Further down the Tyne, the talk might have been of factories or shipyards. Children growing up at Wallsend know that their grandparents, in 1906, built the Mauretania, the fastest liner in the world. At North Shields at the mouth of the river, or on Wearside, memories are about fishing or the work of tugmen and sailors. Further west, into the Pennines, memories of lead mines, quarrying or hill farming prevail.

These traditions, and the feelings which accompany them, though they provide people with common ways of remembering, do not override real differences among them – those of place, occupation, opinion and class. Nor is the tradition coherent or tidy or static.

*

USING THE PAST

The collective past has both general and particular aspects, and the same division helps explain the different ways in which it has been and can be used. That general amalgam of fact, legend and belief which is the history of the North-East is a varied resource culled and used in many diverse ways. It can be parcelled as 'real history' and told to children in schools; it can be sold to tourists as pamphlets on this and that, or it can be reformulated and presented in drama or in song. One of the dramatic successes of the 1960s, discussed in Chapter 4 by Alan Plater, was the play *Close the Coalhouse Door*, with its richly poignant songs by Alex Glasgow. One hundred years before, Joe Wilson, the great Tyneside songwriter and popular entertainer, evoked a distinctive version of it in his song, 'Wor Geordey's Lokil Hist'ry' (*Tyneside Songs and Drolleries*). The song starts with 'Joolyis Seize-her', who came north after he 'konker'd' the Cockneys. It ends with Newcastle itself, 'a toon that we cannet but luk on wi' pride'. Its famous sons – Grainger, Armstrong, George Stephenson (whom Joe describes as 'king o' the world's clivor fellows') – have given it a worldwide reputation. In a reference to the Venerable Bede's monastery at Jarrow, Wilson jests: 'The Jarrow lads noo show'd the way te bild churches'. The song recalls the Roman, Viking and Norman invasions but ends on a note of deep regional pride and praise for the fine architecture of Newcastle itself. His audiences could recognise themselves in his performances. Wilson played back to them idealised versions of a distinctive past, and, through that, strengthened collective identities.

Such general versions of the past and the stories they contain generally have no other purpose to them than to sketch out the contours of the region's history, and are contained within a range of different genres. Some of the tales are heroic, like that of the story of Grace Darling, the Bamburgh girl who rowed her lifeboat in dangerous seas. Others are epic. The story of the rise of the North-East to industrial greatness is, as we shall see, the overarching epic theme. The image of the 'Iron North' captures it well and takes on clear personal forms in the region's heroes. These include the great engineers, like George and Robert Stephenson, Charles Parsons and Lord Armstrong. It includes great scientists like Robert Swan and artists like Thomas Bewick. It also includes the popular heroes like the Tyne Rower, Harry Clasper, or Jackie Milburn, the foot-balling pit lad from Ashington. It includes singers like Joe Wilson, Tommy Armstrong and Ned Corvan. The list is a long one, and, even when the characters are fictional, they contribute in their own way to the collective portrait.

Since the experience of one generation necessarily differs from that of its predecessor, the meaning of the past is something which is constantly reworked. And this leads to versions of the past which strive for a greater coherence, specificity and purpose. The past under some circumstances can then be recalled as a weapon, as a way of making sense of quite specific experiences and struggles so that it becomes a guide to action. Sid Chaplin, one of the region's

greatest writers, sensed this well in a powerful essay about what
was one of the most important annual events in the region, the
Durham Miners' gala. The essay, 'Larks Sang on Banner Day',
reproduced in *In Blackberry Time* (1987), engages the mood and
meaning of the gala and is as heavy in historical symbolism as the
event itself. Chaplin saw it as a commemoration of past struggles.
He recalled in the essay speeches by Jimmy Maxton, 'Wee Ellen
Wilkinson' and Clement Attlee, a 'dry little man', Chaplin wrote,
'who would head the greatest reforming government in British
history.' Their speeches, he believed, bore out the truth of St Paul's
dictum that 'all things are possible through faith'. And his essay
ends, as does the gala itself, with banners being carried into
Durham Cathedral. 'The moment is most solemn. There is a rustle
as the vast congregation rises with one accord. St Cuthbert's folk
have come to pay their respects again.' His view was that, in its
'unrepentant mixture of fun and seriousness, of reunion and celebration', the gala achieved a great sense of family among miners
and mining folk. In his view – and this was his key message – it was
kinship deeply rooted in the most fundamental human values.
What he was acutely conscious of, however, was change.

In another essay, 'A Credo', written in 1964 and republished in
1987, he revealed that: 'All the values I respect came from mining
villages and mining folk, not other writers . . .'. And he went on:

> But the future lies in the cities, great masses of roads and houses and
> factories, great masses of newly affluent people. How will the old
> working-class virtues stand up to city life? What will wither and what
> will die and what, on the other hand, will flower?

Throughout his fiction, Sid Chaplin explored these questions. He
was a man fascinated by the courage and ingenuity of working-
class people. He never lost his belief that, in adversity, Durham
mining folk had found ways to realise the best of what human
beings are capable of.

What concerned him, though, was what the contribution of the
new working class would be. 'Those millions in Coronation streets
and multi-storey flats and council estates', he wrote, represented
'an unexplored continent as far as fiction is concerned', and his fear
was that their response to their world might not match the human
achievement of the old working class. Others in this volume have
probed particular elements of the kinds of changes which worried

Sid Chaplin – changes in city life and culture, in patterns of urban living, in art and drama, the massive alterations in the lives of women and in the ways in which the political culture and institutions of the region have adjusted to the new economic forces at work.

This vortex of change will necessarily alter the prevailing sense of the past which is such a central component of regional culture. People from the new working class who so intrigued Sid Chaplin now shop in the Metro Centre. Those among them in employment – particularly, as David Byrne points out in Chapter 2, those from families with two wage-earners – have never had it so good. Young women from those burgeoning housing estates have a spending power and a freedom their mothers never dreamed of. And to be poor is to be marginalised. Chaplin's 'unexplored continent' stands yet to be discovered. Its remembered past, constantly redefined, requires new interpretations. Drama, as Alan Plater shows in Chapter 4, is part of it. So, too, is humour. And so is sport. 'Gazza', as Harvey Taylor shows in Chapter 7, alters our view of Jackie Milburn in the 1950s and the world *he* represented. The meaning of the past alters with change. And as the worlds of working people become more diverse, as the older solidarities break up, their sense of their past will change and with it their sense of the possibilities for the future.

What is remembered depends on context and occasion. In the 'post-industrial', 'post-urban' North-East, memories have become commoditised and turned to good business. In the process, they may well have become sanitised. Take the Beamish Open-Air Industrial Museum in County Durham; half a million visitors every year go there to see the drift mine, the farm, the reconstructed Methodist chapel, the colliery terrace, the pithead gear and the Co-operative store. It was Museum of the Year in 1987. Now, however, time has stopped at Beamish. The year is 1913, the year in which the Durham coalfield reached its peak. That year 41,532,890 tons of coal were produced by a labour force of 165,807 men and boys. Visitors to the Museum, thousands of whom are from Geordieland itself and who travel there in their cars, are invited to share an experience, the 'Beamish experience'.

Take the young man leading the tourists into the drift mine: he is dressed as he might have been in 1913. His breeches hang just below his knee and his red sweat cloth is hitched to his waist. His is an underground tale of thin seams, cruel owners, hard work, danger and low wages. He has no trouble eliciting the sympathy of his audience. 'Eh,' they say, 'times were bad'.

Who is this young man? A guide or a storyteller? He does both well, and his story is told in a version of the Geordie accent – west Durham pitmatic – almost incomprehensible even to the locals in his audience. Like his workmates in the reconstructed pithead or the reconstructed farm or grocery store, his act is worth seeing. But it is not just his act. He did not write the script. The script is an amalgam, a distillation of well-told tales, which themselves are drawn from a common stock of memory and feeling. His re-enactment of these is a ritual endorsement of their importance and their power. History here is literally spectacular, a drama in a theme park straining credibility to become a village where none previously existed.

The recollection of the bad old days is something which is evoked in one way at an open-air museum, but it is something quite different when it is mobilised in a bitter political struggle like the miners' strike of 1984-5, with its slogan 'SAVE OUR PITS! SAVE OUR COMMUNITIES!' In such an atmosphere, memories of a bitter past were deployed actively to articulate the goals of the National Union of Mineworkers throughout the strike. The miners played on an image of themselves as the most violently oppressed section of the working class. The bitterness of their memories of the 1920s shaped their understanding of their experiences of the pit closures and redundancies of the 1980s. The rich emotional core of those memories, centred on the community itself, was what supplied miners and their families with the inner resources they needed to organise their campaign.

A particularly interesting manifestation of all this is the new Mining Museum at Woodhorn Colliery, Ashington. In the heart of what once was the Northumberland coalfield, in what was once the biggest pit village in the world, this new museum was opened officially in April 1989 by the leader of the Labour Party, the Rt Hon. Neil Kinnock MP. By August of the same year, the Museum had attracted 11,000 visitors, and it is clearly set fair to join Beamish as a popular tourist attraction. Until recently, its most distinctive feature was its display of paintings by the Ashington group of painters who, from the late 1930s onwards, painted themselves into the catalogue of twentieth-century British art by portraying the life and times of their mining village. Now, however, the main exhibits are in the recently opened trade union building. Here is set out the history of the miners' unions. Their banners are displayed, their leaders' lives set out for all to read about. The powerful music of their brass bands plays in the background and, in the images of conflict stretching back to the early 1800s which form the core of the display, the strike of 1984-5 takes pride of place. It is as if nearly two hundred years of struggle had led to this. All the ingredients of a tale well told are there: struggle, fortitude, solidarity and, above all, community, the key to it all. This is a museum with a message. Miners from Ashington helped design it; they supplied photographs and artefacts. Those who work there clearly intend their visitors to learn something, and to understand. The contrast with Beamish is palpable. One museum trades on spectacle and nostalgia, the other has a much more obvious and contemporary political message.

The memories of 1984-5 are now part of a larger pattern, just as are those of the closure of shipyards, steel mills or factories. The Consett Photo Archive has found its place in the annals of British photography in the way its members charted the demise of their steel town. Their work stands as a symbol of a culture and the story of a defeat. It, too, is finding its place in the way in which the past of this region can be evoked and retold with a sharp political edge. Once more, the contrast with the forms of representation of the past which are meant to be consumed as part of leisure and those with a clear political purpose stand out.

At Beamish, the bad old days become a bench mark against which to measure progress and bask in the heartwarming glow of a nostalgic past. It is one free of the squalor, the tensions and the defeats. It is free, too, of the hard graft and steady political gains which were also part of that past and which, in the tedium of committee work in trade unions or branch meetings of the Labour Party or the Co-operative store, even of the chapel, people were encouraged to take their destiny in their own hands with the promise of a better world to be built.

What unites the various strands of the broader regional pattern is a richly textured sense of a hard-worked past, whose marks evoke not only bitterness and poverty, but the greatness, too, of industrial achievement and the pride that went with it. The stories, legends, myths and moral tales encoded in that past are a vast store of ideas

GEORDIES

and images, thoughts and feelings through which poeple in these parts acquire and restate their past. They are the ways and means by which the identities of Geordies are made. Sometimes, however, they are reflections of how others have seen the region and its people. Travellers and social commentators from the beginnings of the nineteenth century through to the present – J. B. Priestley's *English Journey*, though not a novel, is a good example of this kind of writing, as is John Newsom's report, from 1936, *Out of the Pit* – have observed what the people who lived in the North-East might not themselves have felt it necessary to comment on. Then there are the novelists – A. J. Cronin with his evocative tale *The Stars Look Down* (1935), and J. C. Grant's appallingly overdrawn portrait of squalor in mining districts, *The Back-to-Backs*, published in 1930 – which, along with a whole genre of sympathetic left-wing writing about the working class in the 1930s, provided their readers with a sharp image of the brutality of unemployment and the Depression. Dimly reflected back, such accounts, filtering through political commentary, newspaper reporting and popular political action – the Jarrow March is a good, if ambiguous example – held up a mirror in which it was claimed the people of the region could see themselves.

A sense of the past may be handed down from one generation to the next, but it is never merely given (see Figure 9.2). The task of understanding it, of interpreting it, centres on the need to relate it to the circumstances in which it is invoked and the reasons for doing so. Most of the time, most people live their lives in the present tense with a weather eye on the future. The past becomes important only at particular times and in particular circumstances and in each of these in particular ways.

Weddings, births, deaths and anniversaries provide everyday opportunities to recall the past and bring it to order. Such events, in the context of family life, underscore a sense of continuity. The photographs which are part of it become, inevitably, symbols of it and grist to the mill of a family's memory. Civic rituals, armistice day parades, royal occasions and public anniversaries offer similar opportunities to reflect and to recall in ways which bind the past to the present and lend significance to daily lives. Goose fairs, agricultural shows, Lord Mayor's parades, miners' galas (in Durham) and picnics (in Northumberland), festivals, summer exhibitions and pageants can all be seen in this light. They are the occasions on which prevailing versions of the past are ritually endorsed and on

FIGURE 9.2: 'A sense of the past may be handed down from one generation to the next, but it is never merely given.' *Food kitchen* (1920s), Photograph: South Tyneside Libraries.

which the meaning of the past is revealed. That meaning is sometimes a moral tale of solidarity. Miners' galas fall into this group. Pageants emphasise historical continuity. Local fairs emphasise community and the rural traditions which some people like to feel are at the heart of their national identity. The Tyneside Summer Exhibition of 1929, with its oft-recalled African Village, celebrated imperial leadership and the moral superiority of the white man. In each of these instances, the context in which the past is called up is relaxed and congenial, though this was by no means true of the historical realities evoked.

At Beamish, people come to the end of their visit in the museum shop, where they can buy tokens to remind them of the place. They can buy a miner's lamp, some cinder toffee, a piece of carved coal or a humorous booklet on the Geordie past, each of them a comfortable symbol of continuity. The local author and art critic, Scott Dobson, struck a rich seam in nostalgia in the 1960s and 1970s with his booklet, 'Larn Yersel Geordie'. There are many others now in the same genre which, in a good-humoured, self-mocking way, project a regional image which is archaic, eccentric, thoroughly working-class, incorrigibly cheeky and wholly without pain. What it all amounts to is something to be debated. Woodhorn and Beamish both evoke the past in ways which their visitors approve of. Both museums hold up mirrors in which their North-Eastern visitors can recognise some part of themselves. All the elements are there: the poss tubs for washing clothes, pithead baths, allotments, open drains in the back streets, women in pinnies and headscarves, colliery rows, brass bands, lodge banners, flat irons, clippy mats, pigeon lofts and whippets, working men's clubs and chapels, thin seams and the smell of Sunday dinner. This, however, though not to the same degree as at Woodhorn, at least not yet, is history in aspic. The world it evokes is cosy, a world of poor but honest people, of rough diamonds with hearts of gold. But it is a world without the pain of poverty, ignorance or squalor. The museums make no comment on the quality of family life. Women and children are written out of this history; their role is on the sidelines of exploitation rather than where it was actually played out, right at the heart of it. Woodhorn, however, is special in that its new exhibit attaches great significance to the role of women in the support groups during the 1984-5 miners' strike. Generally, though, history is presented through frosted glass. Its shape is recognisable but the detail that matters is blurred. Above all, it is history without action, history without effort.

RECOVERING THE PAST

The past is not just given. It is something to be recovered and reconstituted. And this is not just a normal process, the unfolding work of historians, which goes on when all else is changing. It is much more active than that and has a very different purpose. Whereas historians recover the past to explain how it was, or to test a theory, or to join a debate, the past of popular memory has often been constructed for discrete political ends. And it is recovered, whether in the interests of particular organisations or of private individuals, for very similar reasons – to make sense of the present, to legitimate a course of action, but above all to provide for coherence and continuity in the way people make sense of their interests and their lives.

Sometimes this is clear and obvious, as in the case of the recovery of the history of mineworkers in the nineteenth century and in the early years of the present century. It is less obvious, though no less purposeful, in the case of the 'Iron North' story, which is retold in various ways to assert the qualities of a region which too often in the past has suffered from a poor industrial and cultural image. Here, the concern with image, evident in the 1930s Special Areas legislation but particularly evident in the regional policies of the 1960s, is to find a positive way to portray the region to attract inward investment and diversify the regional economy. Both attempts to recover the region's past have contributed potent elements to the bricolage of popular memory in these parts.

The history of the history of miners in the North-East is a telling example of the way in which popular memory is structured. In his foreword to the 1971 edition of *The Miners of Northumberland and Durham* by Richard Fynes, first published in 1873, Lord Shinwell ('Manny' Shinwell, former MP for the Durham mining village of Easington) recalled how, after the First World War, while engaged in propaganda work in Durham, he first heard of Fynes's book. Old miners recalled for him the harsh details of life and labour in mining villages. They told him of slave-like working conditions, starvation wages, of the imposition of fines for alleged offences, of 'frequent pit disasters, even excessive brutality by police against striking miners'. These conversations helped him understand the 'built-in bitterness among miners, their distrust of coal owners and colliery officials'. It helped him, he said, understand their sensitivity to the first history of their industry.

What interested Shinwell in Fynes's account were the disclosures which portrayed

> the courage, the unselfish and heroic behaviour, the fortitude and the readiness to endure the most extreme perils and hardship by men who sought to create a better life for the oppressed mineworkers and their families; some who gave their lives for their comrades and were undaunted in their principles.

The period addressed in this passage, the period after the First World War, was one of considerable change in the mining industry. The histories Shinwell heard when he toured Durham in those years were stories which made legitimate what was then the miners' most central demand of government – the nationalisation of the industry. The past was being deployed here to alter the present; it was being shaped in a particular way for a particular political context. It was being drawn in a way which contrasted squalor, greed and inefficiency with the promise of planning, justice and welfare, benefits which were widely believed to be the outcome of nationalisation. In Shinwell's encounter with Fynes's history, the future meets the past.

Lord Shinwell's foreword was written in 1970 during the faltering days of a Labour government. His special stress on the unselfishness of an older generation of miners must be read, I believe, against the background of debates within the Labour Party during the late 1960s over incomes policy. Miners then were in the vanguard of demands from the well-organised working class for higher wages. In defence of policies requiring the well-organised to hold down their demands to enable governments to protect, as they saw it, the real incomes of the poor and preserve high levels of public expenditure on services, Fynes's history was called to political service. In Shinwell's report, we find the rich ingredients of a potent image – struggle, exploitation, fortitude and principle. It is an image which Fynes himself intended younger members of the union to appreciate because it underlined the importance of responsible attitudes and close cooperation between masters and men. Only through responsible industrial relations could mineworkers, Fynes believed, improve their lot. His evocation of a terrible past was very much intended to convey how much things had improved, vindicating for the present generation the political methods which he believed had brought improvement about.

In 1907, another history of the Durham Miners' Association was published. Written by John Wilson, one of the union leaders, at the request of one of the Durham lodges, Wilson was clear that his book was to show younger men 'the conditions we have come from, the toil and anxiety those who were the initiators had to face, and the large amount of unremunerative labour they had to perform'. His concern for the younger generation was also clear:

> Our present position has been bought with a price, the amount of which is unknown to this generation, many of whom are like the prodigal, who inheriting a fortune and knowing nothing of the hardships involved in the accumulation, squanders with indifference that which has cost bitter years and hardship.

The context in which this remark has to be read is that of the growth of Labour politics throughout the coalfield, particularly of the Independent Labour Party and of the fear which men like Wilson had that radical political thinking might undermine the conciliatory traditions of the county. Like their liberal counterparts in Northumberland, what the Durham leaders feared was the emergence of a socialist class-consciousness among their members.

W. P. Richardson, then Durham Miners' agent, wrote in the foreword to the 1923 edition of Fynes's book that 'This is a wonderful story, revealing the hard and tragic life of the Miner and his family during the early part of the nineteenth century'. The book was first republished in 1923 when, explained Mr Richardson, 'there is a very grave danger of the Northern Miner, especially the younger generation, forgetting the past history of our industry, and with it our indebtedness to those noble pioneers who so faithfully, and at great personal sacrifice and privation, fought and toiled so that the greater liberty we now enjoy might be won'. On this reading of the past, it is the values of personal integrity and sacrifice which win out in the end, not the politics of class confrontation which were emerging strongly through the Miners' Federation of Great Britain.

The point is this: history is a resource to fuel political debate. Some of the most potent images of the deprivations of mining communities, which are so much part of the popular memory of the North-East, were formed in the political struggles of the miners' unions themselves. The reality they sought to evoke was unquestionably harsh. When miners from previous generations, like those of today, recalled those times, they did so with a justified sense of pride that much had been done to overcome them. Nevertheless, the foundations of their beliefs were sunk not in hard historical facts but in the political interpretation of those facts. The history of the history of miners is no different in this respect from that of engineers, steelmen, seamen or agricultural labourers, except, of course, in that, at least in the North-East, there are many more histories of miners than of any other group.

The histories of organised labour in the North-East are essentially about men. Women have been largely excluded from the record, as Elaine Knox has shown in Chapter 6. When women have written about the past, however, their writing has often had a similar rationale: to instruct the young in the sober virtues of hard work as the only way to a better world. The domestic past or the world of childhood is invariably recalled, both in print and in memory, in ways which underline its relentless labour – its bread-making, its matmaking, cooking on open fires, its street lamp games and simple pleasures. 'We were poor, but we were happy' is the organising sentiment.

The genre of such recall has to be carefully noted. Mary Wade's account of her childhood in Bedlington in the 1920s and 1930s is typical; *To the Miner Born* conjures up her childhood world in a way meant to instruct young readers of today. 'Today's children,' she writes, 'find it difficult to imagine a typical washing day of the early 1900s. Very often there had to be a combination of washing and baking on the same day, especially in the larger-family homes.' Much of the book strikes this note; later, for example, she notes that 'During my childhood, it was interesting to see the ways by which people could put their spare time to good use'. Her record of the achievements of Bedlington District Council, of which she was a member, is a hymn to public conscience and worthy causes, a celebration of steady social progress, a moral tale.

Mary Wade's history is simultaneously local and regional. People from Bedlington will recognise the people she wrote about. But people from all over the industrial North-East, particularly the mining districts, will recognise her account. For what she is retelling is a tale everyone knows; those with roots in the region can identify in their own family histories the same ingedients. The further the region moves from its heavy industrial past, the more these tales are steeped in nostalgia and regret and the more they frame that sense of loss which many older people will talk about. A good example of this is a pamphlet, *But the World Goes On the Same*, written in 1979 and published by a local radical publishing group, the Strong Words Collective, which for a short while published pamphlets on changing social conditions in Durham mining villages, drawing heavily on the techniques of oral history. Much of this writing has a strong undertow of regret and is suffused with an image of how there has been a terrible decline between the past and the present. Ron Rooney, one of the miners interviewed, put it this way:

Things have changed a lot though. In the pit community you could leave your back door open. You never locked your doors at night. Folks came and folks went out. On a weekend when they came away from the clubs and pubs, you used to have sing-songs in the streets. Everybody joined in, everybody knew everybody. But as the mines went the community went too. Although there's some good community spirit on the housing estates, it's not what it was in the mining villages.

Mr Rooney was not revealing historical truth here; yet there is a truth in what he said, and it is a powerful one. It is one which connects him to his own past, validating again those values to which he holds most strongly.

But there are other emotions, too, which are inseparable from the way in which the past is recalled. Of particular importance is pride. One very fine example of this was provided again by Sid Chaplin, who wrote the text for a series of illustrated articles for the *Newcastle Evening Chronicle* in October 1969 on the theme of 'The Iron North'. These special supplements to the evening paper contained headlines like: 'THEY BUILT THE WORLD'S BIGGEST SHIPS, THE WORLD'S MOST POWERFUL GUNS: THEY PRODUCED HUGE QUANTITIES OF THE WORLD'S FINEST COAL'. Chaplin wrote of a region that, building magnificence on magnificence, 'had been, if not all-exclusively, the "brain tank" of the nation during a great period of flowering which lasted roughly from 1800 to the early 1900s'. It was all made possible, he argued, by a 'brilliant generation of colliery managers and pit engineers'. In a passage referring to the region's engineers, he had this to say:

> If the North-East was an Empire within an Empire then what centurions it raised – Palmer, the founders of Hawthorne Leslie; Clarke Chapman; Swan Hunter and Wigham Richardson; Merz, Reyrolle, to name only a few. And each had its legion of workmen who included incomparable engineering craftsmen.

A feature worth noting of Chaplin's comments is that they evoked a past which now no longer exists. It was disappearing rapidly in the late 1960s, and the pace of change did not slacken. His was a celebration in which all Geordies could share, and, when he wrote these words, those seeking to attract new industry to a failing economy would have been well pleased with him. For here is an image of creativity without conflict, craftsmanship without class, or hardship endured with pride and of human sensitivities tempered to tolerance and kindness. It amounts, perhaps, to a notion of a regional identity which transcends those of class and is in this respect a very different way of talking about the place compared to the social and political commentary of the 1930s.

Pride, regret, nostalgia and solidarity are all part of a structure of feeling about the past which is widely shared in the North-East. Such feelings are sharp and real because the reality they evoke is passing by. A new kind of society has emerged, particularly in the period since the Second World War and with great speed from the 1970s. The older industries have all but collapsed. The communities they supported have been uprooted. Old skills have become redundant. New industry has come to the North-East: light industry, industry from abroad and the remarkable growth of a service sector. Government itself, both local and national, is now a major employer. The North-East has a high rate of inward investment from the Far East, from Japan and from the United States. Suburbs have outgrown the cities, and towns and new estates eclipse the older council estates as desirable places to live. A relatively high degree of regional isolation has been eroded through both inward and outward migration, the growth of mass consumer industries, the spread of television and road networks. The continuities – of community, of the mining village, of the densely packed terraces of Scotswood or Wallsend, of trade union branches, of Labour politics and, above all, of heavy industry – have been broken.

THE PAST IN THE FUTURE

In the transition from the old to the new, the old has been revalued. How the past is imagined has altered and, like all processes of memory, the re-evaluation has been selective. It will always be selective. That is how popular memory works; it is the only way it can meet the emotional needs of the present and deal with the dilemmas and contradictions which people experience in their daily lives. Each new generation has to live the past differently.

The need for this is not, however, just a matter of anthropological fact. It is much more a question of practice and intention, of the way in which people seek deliberately to locate themselves in time and draw appropriate conclusions from what they take their history to be. They need such insight to understand and clarify their goals and to understand their own experience. The recovery of the past from the 1870s onwards was a task shaped largely by the need felt among organised working men in heavy industries to articulate their political goals. That effort produced the image which still prevails in popular memory – the image of hardship overcome. But it is now, with the exception of those in the mining districts who lived through the 1984-5 strike, a politically sanitised image, free of the doubts and differences from which it was formed. And what it provides for people is a kind of caricature but one in which, nevertheless, people from the North-East can recognise themselves.

The memories which are part of the history are therefore selective. They invariably relate to the experience of well-organised groups of male workers. Save perhaps in rural Northumberland or West Durham, there is little in popular memory which acknowledges much of the lives of agricultural labourers. Women are largely written out of the script, though this is altering. The history of Britain as a whole, of the rise of industry, the World Wars, Fascism or the protracted demise of Empire, which required, even into the 1960s, large numbers of young men from the region to fight in foreign parts, is not part of it. Of course people can recall the Blackshirts or the Jarrow March; they can remember Churchill and the Second World War. Thousands of North-Eastern women can recall their days in munitions factories and shipyards or their work on the land. Those thousands of young girls who were sent 'to place' in the 1930s as domestic servants are beginning to tell and to have their stories told. But fact is one thing, experience is another. Both require interpretation. The interpretive frameworks of popular memory remain stubbornly those of the older, organised working class. It is these which, for now, lend meaning and significance to how people think about themselves and their future.

The tragedy in all of this, of course, is that such imagery is no longer vital. It is eminently exploitable in the industries which grow on nostalgia, but it provides diminishing resources from which people can make sense of their present experience. The North-East is a rapidly changing region. Its social and cultural contours no longer follow those of heavy industrial investment and the extractive industries. Prewar, women provided less than one-fifth of the region's labour force; now it is almost one-half. Manufacturing industry in the region employed over a third of the region's labour in 1971; the figure is now down to about a fifth, with the service sector accounting for close on seventy per cent of all employment. Once upon a time, the region had its own capitalists; now it is an outpost for the capitalists from abroad. But not just from abroad; all those Geordies with pension funds and insurance policies, certainly those with their penny's worth of shares in privatised but formerly nationalised industries, are capitalists of a kind.

Under such circumstances, the fear is that older solidarities will be forgotten or turned into nostalgia, for there's money in that. County Durham has been turned, ludicrously, into 'The Land of the Prince Bishops'; South Tyneside, in an ingenious piece of publicity, has become 'Catherine Cookson Country'. And Northumberland has become a national park, known for its archaeology, its Border castles, wild, open moor and dramatic seascapes. It is almost as if the Industrial Revolution and the twentieth century bypassed us. The image-makers are reaching deeply back in time to an earlier, less contentious past, where the divisions and conflicts now built into the architecture of looted monasteries and Border castles no longer have relevance. Certainly, this particular past is wholly irrelevant to the issues which capitalist industrialisation produced and with which, too often unwittingly, industrialists, trade unionists, workers of all kinds, governments and families are still struggling. These are the issues of justice and fairness, of a decent life for all and of the best means to achieve these things. The history built into memory, now wrapped up in a marketable nostalgia, was made, in part, to achieve these things.

That history, and perhaps, too, the popular memory which it helped form, though it is too early yet to tell, will be defined in different ways as the present overtakes the past and the outlines of a new future become clearer. The subtle transfer of the past from one generation to the next takes a different form in the suburban housing estate of mobile people from the form it took in the mining village or between father and son in a shipyard. On the other hand, through education, the mass media, better transport and the revolution in communications, people can talk to one another in ways which the likes of Richard Fynes, John Wilson, W. P. Richardson, Mary Wade and hundreds of others could hardly have imagined possible. But what will they say to one another? What stories will they tell? What victories and what defeats will they celebrate? What structures of feeling will they evoke? Who will recover the past? For whom will it matter? In what contexts will it matter? Who will define a future? (See Figure 9.3.) What ends will they hope to achieve? What will be forgotten?

FIGURE 9.3: 'Who will recover the past? For whom will it matter? In what contexts will it matter? Who will define a future?' *Jarrow Crusade, 1986 version* (1986), Photograph: South Tyneside Libraries.

The questions are open, but the answers are even now being worked on. They have to be. It is a matter not of choice but of necessity. The answers will out; images will confront experience and, as new, perhaps brighter futures are forged, the past itself will change. It will do so, it is to be hoped, not on a note of maudlin regret but with a new sense discovery and hope, where the new past will not be the property of the big battalions of organised male labour, or sealed up as heritage in museums or the promotional literature of development corporations, but will reflect the stresses and textures of the lives of a much more diverse region. And since the means through which the discoveries can be framed and communicated are infinitely richer than they once were, there is at least a promise of a dialogue in which different pasts can be compared, refined, expressed and lived.

CHAPTER TEN
Coda

PAUL L. YOUNGER

' "Geordies could end up like Red Indians, as extras in films
about the North-East." '
(Unemployed shipyard welder, quoted by
Robert Chesshyre, *The Return of a Native Reporter*, 1987)

'WHEREVER YE GAN ya boond te find a Geordie' – that's what the
song says. Or, as me Granda told me, 'Divvent worry. There's
Geordies aall ower the place. If ya feelin' lonely when ye're away,
just whistle the Blaydon Races an' some bugger'll join in.'

I must admit I was having my doubts about this theory, standing
at the edge of an intertribal powwow in Oklahoma – the only white
face in a crowd of several hundred Indians. I was a guest of Larry
Roman Nose (Southern Cheyenne) and his family; I wasn't even
going to bother whistling the Blaydon Races, it would have been
out of time with the drums anyway. Out of the circling crowd of
dancers, a young woman in a Kiowa dance costume approached
me. 'Where are you from?' she asked. I always had trouble in
answering this question to Americans. If they hazarded a guess, it
was usually Ireland or Scotland, never England. The English, you
see, talk and behave like Alastair Cooke. For my part, I found
myself unable to describe myself as English. 'Northumbrian' or
Geordie is how I feel, but my American friends had never heard of
Northumbria. So, to this young Kiowa woman, her features as
Indian as the powwow songs, I gave the usual garbled answer:

'Aa'm from Northumbria, which is next to Scotland, but currently
governed as part of England.' What a mouthful.
To my surprise, the Kiowa lass said: 'Eeh! Whereabouts?'

'Why Hebburn, near Newcastle.'
'Never. Me Mam lives in Jesmond!'

And it turned out her father was a full-blooded Kiowa, her mother a Geordie 'GI Bride'. God forgive me for ever doubting my Granda; he knew what he was on about.

Growing up in Hebburn Quay in the early 1960s, there was always someone 'away for work'. There was one uncle in the Merchant Navy, and another settling back home from the sea, in accordance with my Granda's preconditions on the hand of his daughter in marriage. His own enforced travels had convinced my Granda that a husband in the cokeworks was worth two in the navy. He had missed the boats at Dunkirk by a fortnight, and had crossed Normandy to escape, only to join a frigate which was promptly sunk by a torpedo in the Irish Sea. What the Elmfield Club (CIU) might lack in excitement, it made up for in safety.

Besides the merchant mariners, there was an entire host of great aunties and uncles scattered about London, economic exiles all, whose frequent visits home occasioned some of the finest 'hooleys' I can remember. Because of my Mam's abilities as a singer and pianist, our house was often the venue for these great family gatherings, and I can remember the repertoire to the last note. Each of the family elders would take it in turn to start a song. At the beginning of the evening, the favourites were the light-hearted Geordie and Irish songs: 'Keep Your Feet Still, Geordie Hinnie', 'Cushy Butterfield', 'Phil the Fluter's Ball'. But as the hours and the whisky wore on, the sad songs of exile would come to the fore: 'Mother Machree'. 'Danny Boy', 'The Eriskay Love-lilt', 'How are things in Glocamorra?' – lumps in the throat all round, and tears in the eyes of the shipyard men, their calloused hands on the shoulders of their loved ones who'd be leaving again in the morning.

For my own generation, the pattern of departures and emotional reunions continues. My eldest sister has now been 'away for work' in the darkest South for a decade; three of my cousins are scattered from Saudi to Sydney in HM Armed Forces; many of my mates from school are exiled in the 'Home Counties'. It's funny, isn't it, the 'Home Counties'? None of this lot feel at home there at all; for them, 'home' means the North-East, and if anything 'County' means that hotel opposite Newcastle Central Station.

The frequent homecomings are always an excuse to indulge in the great Geordie pastime of looking back. With bottles of 'Dog'

(what the white settlers call Newky Brown) on the table, labels
facing outwards like badges of merit, we remake pre-Poulson Tyneside: back lanes, ballast hills, outdoor toilets (netties), pigeon crees;
the ferries, the cranes, Swan's, Leslie's, Palmer's; the pit heaps,
Rising Sun, The Betty, 'Cotia Pit – not forgetting Wyn Davies,
Supermac and the Leazes Choir. But most of all the incomparable
'daft laughs' of days gone by. Then just as we're starting to get too
soppy, there's always someone ready to bring us down to earth,
either by humming the 'Hovis' tune or else telling us straight:
'Haway, man, you lot, yiz are as soft as clarts'.

Under conditions such as these, we rarely get to speculate on the
future. There's not as much to say, anyway. We know we'll agree
on the gap between what we want and what experience tells us to
expect. It's easier, and often a lot more satisfying, to just vent your
spleen instead:

'Aa canna stand the bliddy Tories me, especially that Trotter.'

'Divvent taalk te me aboot Neville Trotter!'

'Ha' ye seen the graffiti in the bogs? It says "Make Tories wear
blobs".'

'That could be physically impossible.'

'Aa think we should rebuild Hadrian's Wall along the Tees and
get shot o' the lot o' them.'

'The Tees is ower far man. The Wear's nearer the mark.'

'Howld on man, Aa've got mates in Peterlee!'

Not that this patter is only heard during homecomings. Remember, wherever ye gan ya boond te find a Geordie. Since the 1920s,
people have been leaving the North-East at rates of 5,000 (in the
1970s) to 80,000 (1927-8) a year. The net loss continues, with the
South-East remaining the most frequent destination (fifty-four per
cent) for emigrants. For the figures, look at A. R. Townsend's
'Incomers and returned emigrants' (Working Paper 45, Durham
University 1977) and the Tyne and Wear Research and Intelli-
gence Unit's 1991 *Migration Report*. In my travels, I have come
across cohesive expatriate Geordie communities in Nottingham-
shire (where refugees from the first 1960s wave of pit closures have
established a club, affiliated, replete with leek shows and Fed
Special) and in north London (where Geordie building workers
have transplanted the traditional Tyneside weekend festivities to
the Great Northern Hotel at King's Cross).

My first stint of living away from Tyneside landed me on the other side of the Atlantic. This circumstance was a combination of the need to find employment and the perceived need to chase a woman. To get the cash, I'd applied to every funding organisation I could find, being careful to substitute geological alibis for my true imperatives, and, with my customary good luck, came up trumps with an academic fellowship. Meeting the other successful applicants in New York was an interesting experience, for they included the first *confident* Tories I had ever met in my life. In the words of the song:

> Once Aa met a Tory,
> doon in Jarra toon,
> man, he looked sae lonely,
> had nee marras roond!
> (To the tune 'Dance to Thy
> Daddy' from Dave Bell)

Even the posh end of Jarrow votes Labour (see Figure 10.1). But here were the Oxbridge lot, as intense as the last minute of bingo at the Buffs, as serious as a red and white scarf in the Gallowgate End, holding forth on the need for 'rationalisation' in British industry. Well, my Dad had just been 'rationalised' out of Swan's a few months before, so I wasn't in much mood for their slavver. And the academic Marxist in their midst wasn't much use either. He gave me the impression that bringing my background to bear in arguments with Tories was a form of intellectual dishonesty, and that if I hadn't obtained my socialist consciousness by serious study and a subscription to *Marxism Today*, then I'd be better keeping quiet. Wish again, bonny lad.

Presently, the Fellows dispersed to their various seats of learning, most of them to do MBAs at Ivy League universities. I took my geological hammer to the ivy-free zone of Oklahoma State University at Stillwater. As there were very few Europeans in town, I was flattered by the curiosity of many American people. Most of the people I met were, naturally enough, white, middle-class students. These people certainly knew how to have fun, and I certainly enjoyed myself but, like many British residents in the USA, I was surprised at how different it is from the UK. The apparent ease of communication is deceptive. We tend to assume that, because we can understand the language, we can also understand the way people think. So, often, the attitudes and feelings of my friends caught me by surprise.

FIGURE 10.1: 'Even the posh end of Jarrow votes Labour.' *Jarrow March* (1936), Photograph: South Tyneside Libraries.

I was even more surprised by the way in which exposure to another culture led me more deeply into my own. Looking back, I saw the North-East with new eyes. I would carefully work over my memories of childhood; sometimes it seemed like I'd made it all up. Even though the poverty of Tyneside stood out in relief from my new perspective, I began to feel genuinely fortunate at having been born there, just in time to experience a Tyneside of shipyards and pits, the industries we built our identity around. Back home, I'd never really felt 'fortunate' to be born in one of the least regarded corners of Britain; at best, the struggle to retain self-respect had given me a sort of prickly pride. Now, though, it was all different. A 'province' became a whole country, neatly contained between the North Sea, the Pennines, the Cleveland Hills and the Cheviots. At the heart of it, Newcastle was the capital, the Tyne Bridge our Arc de Triomphe. The countryside of Northumbria seemed, and does seem, peculiarly matched to the people. There is an austere edge to the beauty of the landscape, and the history of the villages reflects this. The mines may have gone, but the people remain. There is a down-to-earth quality about eastern Durham and south-east Northumberland that is rare, a quality born of that unusual merger of rural and urban life, the industrial village. Stand on Penshaw Hill and look around. The natural landscape of gentle limestone hills would, in the south, be colonised by Cotswold folk; here, the blinking lights of Shiney Row, Hetton, Castletown and the new Nissan factory tell a different tale of settlement and struggle. Even the apparent metropolis of Tyneside is still readily divisible into villages, with variations in accent and dialect every few miles.

In the wild and remote areas, the high Durham Dales and the Cheviots, the atmosphere is just as distinctive. Wandering these hills, in this least populated corner of England (or at least in what the atlases call England), you are still far more likely to meet a shepherd than a tourist. In the ruins of abandoned settlements in the high hopes and cleughs, and in the patterns of former field systems on the braes and haughs, the history of settlement, dispossession and struggle is just as visible as in the pit heaps and terraced rows nearer the coast. Looking back from America, Northumbria, both rural and urban, appeared to me to have been born and brought up in hardship; struggle seemed to be the genetic link between people and place. In my childhood, the very skyline was marked by the symbols of struggle and work, in the form of shipyard cranes and pithead gear. I now saw the renowned friendliness of the Geordies as the fruit of communal responses to hard times. It was never grim faces I recalled when musing on home. With the romantic heart of the exile, it was always the cheerful smiles I remembered, and the pragmatism: 'There's nee shame in poverty, but by hell there's nee glory in it either!'

With such thoughts shaping inside me, I sometimes felt the need for discussion. Given the curiosity so many of my American friends showed about Britain, you could be forgiven for imagining this would not be difficult to arrange. Too often, though, people just wanted to confirm their prejudices about Britain:

'Yeah, you guys have that crazy Monty Py-thon show dontcha? Man, the British sense of humour is *so* weird! ... Say, have you ever met the Queen? ... You are so lucky to have a marvellous leader like Mrs Thatcher ... I hear it rains all the time in your country. Is it always foggy in London?'

Well, this was all very well but, to be honest, I needed a bit more to talk about. Some of the fundamental differences in outlook between my hosts and myself began to come to the fore. If I asked them about their home town, or their home state, they would become puzzled and dismissive: 'What's the big deal? I was born there. Mom and Dad live there. So what?'. Often, the subject of my background would arise from the frequent questions about my accent. I would explain about the variety of regional dialects in England, and the local variations in the Geordie dialect which mean you can often pin someone's origin down to a few square miles on the basis of the words they use and the way they use them. This was astonishing to many Americans, as was the lack of geographical mobility which it implied. In the USA, variations in accent occur over vast distances, and geographical stability is now largely the preserve of conservative ethnic communities on the coasts and in the poorer rural areas. While there are communities which have built a strong identity out of industrial and socialist traditions, particularly in Appalachia, my evolving notions of struggle as the genetic link between my community and its territory were unintelligible to most of my American friends. On reflection, this is not that surprising. I don't imagine these notions would go down very well in Surrey, or in Darras Hall for that matter.

There was one group who didn't find my thoughts quite so unusual. Although many Oklahomans have some Indian blood, it was some time before I met any Indians who were conscious of their tribal identity. This is because the tribal people live predominantly in rural areas, and few of them are to be found in university towns such as Stillwater. My interest in poetry and music, the only true international language, provided the common ground on which I eventually met Indian people. A friend asked me to go to a poetry recital by a Cheyenne poet; I went, listened and liked what I heard. After the recital, I was introduced to the poet, Lance Henson (Mahako Domiuts, or 'Walking Badger' in Cheyenne), and to cut a long story short, that evening ended with Geordie songs and Cheyenne stories winding out into the small hours.

At Lance's invitation, I paid the first of many visits to his home near the Canadian River. There we spent many days talking of religion and politics, place and people, poetry and music. My friendship with Lance provided the key to many more experiences in Indian country; with the Hopi, Dineh (Navajo), Cherokee,

Kiowa and Oglala Sioux; at powwows, in hogans, and, the greatest privilege, at a Lakota Sundance. I was inspired by the vigour with which many of the Indian peoples still adhere to their traditional languages, religions and cultures, despite centuries of repression by the incomers. I learned of the ways and means of Indian resistance; how Pan-Indian unity evolved in the face of the government's most elaborate attempts to deprive Indian children of their heritage. In the paramilitary Bureau of Indian Affairs' boarding schools, Indians of many tribes found out how much they had in common, and developed new ways of working together against their common oppressor. I witnessed Pan-Indian resistance in action, where mining companies, aided and abetted by the federal government, are attempting to drive people off sacred ancestral lands which conceal coal and uranium reserves. To the Cheyenne and their Indian cousins, the notion of struggle linking a people and their land is natural. Indeed, the harsh aspects of their country and its climate, such as the 'badlands', the tornadoes and the violent hailstorms, which are so often feared and resisted by the incomers, are respected and relished by the Indians; they are especially honoured in poetry and song.

All of this made me ever more anxious to examine more closely the notions I had of my own place and my own community. When I got home, I resolved to check the substance of the half-memories which kept surfacing in my mind. To do this, I looked back through Northern history, only this time it was even further back than pre-Poulson Tyneside. I plunged deep into the prehistory of Northumbria, to the hill forts and stone circles, then read my way through the Dark Ages, enlightened by Bede and Y Gododdin. Even in those far-off times, the distinctiveness of the area was apparent. It is remarkable how long the territory of Northumbria has been border country. The Tyne seems to have been the approximate boundary between the Brigantes and the Votadini (neighbouring Celtic tribes, who have left their mark in many place names, including the Tyne, the Cheviot and even Jarrow). Subsequently, the boundary between the Roman Empire and the untamed Celts to the north followed a similar line, preserved in Hadrian's Wall. Later still, the area was the meeting place of Angles and Celts, and ultimately the border lands between England and Scotland. From the long centuries of tension inherent in living at the margins of different cultures, a distinctive hybrid emerged, which persisted, and found its wildest expression in the Border Reivers.

I noted the evidence for the persistence of Celtic culture in Anglian Northumbria: land tenure on the Welsh pattern (so unlike the patterns elsewhere in England that the Domesday Book had to stop short at the Tees); place names (the contemporaneous names for the two Northumbrian provinces, Bernicia and Deira, are themselves Celtic, in distinction to all other Anglian kingdom names); survivals of Welsh personal names into the thirteenth century; and the use of Gaelic as the court language of seventh-century Northumbria. The 'golden age' of the Celtic church in Northumbria remains an inspiration in the religious life of the region even today; indeed, interest in Aidan, Cuthbert, Oswald and the Holy Island of Lindisfarne is enjoying a great resurgence. Aidan seems to me a suitable patron for the region, for he stands out as a great populist. This was a man who went on foot to the remote hamlets in the Cheviots and refused the king's gift of a horse in case it came between him and the ordinary people of Northumbria.

After the long years of the independent kingdom of Northumbria, centralisation came to a head in the wake of the Norman invasion. The subjugation of Northumbria was attempted by a 'scorched-earth' policy, and outbursts of Northumbrian rebellion continued to create problems for a ruling class now centred in southern England, where it was to remain. Next, I read of the brief but colourful interludes of the Rising of the Northern Earls (1569) and the Northumbrian Jacobites (1715). When my attention turned to the nineteenth century, to the stories of Hepburn, Jude and the first stirrings of Northumbrian working-class radicalism, I found myself in inspiring territory. Again, religion found its place at the heart of the struggle, this time in the shape of that self-education and organisation which was wrought by the Primitive Methodist Connexion, a movement which spawned so many of the early trade union leaders.

From my excursion through the histories, I re-emerged to the present day feeling vindicated. In many ways, history supports the notions of Northumbria as a distinctive land and people who have grown together through struggle. Nonetheless, I was still wholly unprepared for the shocks awaiting me at my homecoming. And I'm not just talking about the eighty-five per cent cut in income. From the romance of history, where hardship and struggle can seem noble, I was brought down to earth with a bump. During my absence, unemployment had continued to rise. Now my own father was made redundant once again, and we all knew that this was the end of his working life. Paradoxically, the only new building to have appeared in Jarrow during my absence was a Jobcentre, complete with card racks devoid of adverts. Meanwhile the drone of Thatcher continued, accusing the Geordies of being ungrateful 'moaning minnies'. I looked around at the devastated Tyneside I had returned to, saw the final annihilation of the shipyards on the Wear, watched the demolition of the Naval Yard at Walker, saw the colliery in my home town demolished, and shook my head in disbelief. Many of my friends, relatives and acquaintances were either unemployed or living in constant fear of being made unemployed. The traditionally minded majority of Tyneside, who

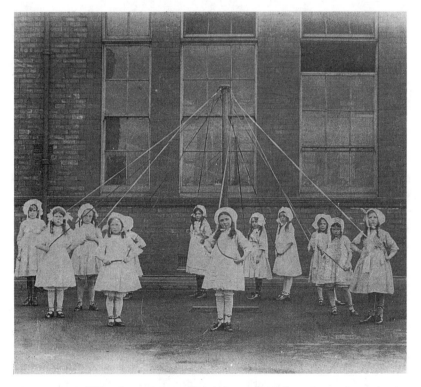

FIGURE 10.2: 'Often it seems we will only be acceptable to those who make the rules if we abandon our language, culture and place of birth.' *Redby School, Fulwell, Sunderland* (c. 1900), Photograph: Newcastle upon Tyne Libraries and Arts.

maintain their beliefs in communitarian principles and retain some pride in their identity as a worthwhile people, were, and are well and truly under attack.

Frequently, my mind flies back to the Plains, for I see problems here comparable to those in Indian country:

- a feeling of isolation from the political decision-making process; the more we vote Labour, the more the government ignores us;
- a feeling of isolation from the dominant culture. Often it seems we will only be acceptable to those who make the rules if we abandon our language, culture and place of birth (see Figure 10.2). For the sake of our human dignity, we must look at ways of defining our own cultural identity;
- a ravaged economy. We are now left in Northumbria with the dying remains of traditional heavy industries, an unstable branch-plant sector, and poorly paid jobs in the service sector.

Increasingly, the Indian response to these problems has been to reclaim their right to self-determination and to re-establish their own forms of tribal government. In this process, the values of traditional Indian religion, language and culture are undergoing a renaissance. Inspired by such visions, I spent my exile years dreaming of Geordie self-determination. Tom Hadaway's Uncle George is right – 'Ye'll nivvor yuk a haddock wirra pen nib' – but Major and his ilk can run, or run down our entire region with the stroke of a pen. We've had too many centuries of rule by pen from London. It's time that Geordie swagger counted for more than cutting a dash in the Bigg Market.

About the Authors

DAVID BYRNE was born in South Shields in 1947 and educated at local Catholic schools, Newcastle University and the London School of Economics. His numerous writings include a recent study of a Tyneside inner-city area. He is Senior Lecturer in Social Policy at the University of Durham, a Labour councillor in Gateshead, and a member of the Tyne and Wear 2000 group.

BARRY CARR is forty-one years old. Married with four children, he has lived on Tyneside all his life. A writer/researcher, he is writing a history of the Shields Arab community – *for which he hopes to find a publisher.*

ROBERT COLLS was born in South Shields. His mother ran the home and worked at the local hospital; his father worked for fifty years as a driller at the ship-repair yard of the Tyne Dock Engineering Company. After the freedom of the streets of Laygate Lane, followed by eleven-plus and university, he worked as a volunteer in the Sudan. He moved with his family to Leicester in 1979. In an otherwise fortunate life, he supports Newcastle United, still keeps his boots clean, and lives in hope. He is currently Visiting Professor of British History at the University of Mississippi.

TOM HADAWAY was born in the dockside area of North Shields. An adopted child, he left school at fourteen to work in the fish trade, and was forty when he started writing for radio, encouraged by the playwright C. P. Taylor. His television work included 'Play for Today' *The Happy Hunting Ground* and the BBC BAFTA entry *God Bless Thee Jackie Maddison.* He also worked on *When the Boat Comes In* and has recently scripted Amber Films' *Seacoal* and *In Fading Light.* He is currently working on a joint UK-Australian television series on the life of a child-migrant.

ELAINE KNOX comes from a long line of Shields mariners and working women. Her matriarchal family and tales from her mother and grandmother gave her a fascination with the North-East's culture and the historical changes of her home town. After eight years as a short-hand typist, she went to Newcastle Polytechnic, leaving three years later with a BA, a hefty overdraft and an interest in real ale. She is at present researching for a PhD at the University of Lancaster, which she hopes will do justice to North-East working women. Although she lives in Preston, Lancashire, she still considers Newcastle to be the capital of England.

BILL LANCASTER was born in Blaydon. After school, he worked in industry for twelve years before starting higher education. He has published books on nineteenth- and twentieth-century urban and social history, and is presently working on the social history of the department store. He teaches modern social history at the University of Northumbria at Newcastle.

ALAN PLATER was born in Jarrow in 1935 and now lives in North London. He has been a full-time writer since 1960 and has accumulated many awards – including the Writers' Guild of Great Britain and the Sony award for his radio plays, and the Royal Television Society, BAFTA and the Broadcasting Press Guild for his television work, most notably *A Very British Coup, Fortunes of War* and the *Beiderbecke* series. His novel *Misterioso* appeared in a screen version on BBC TV. When he remembers where he left his spare time, he spends it listening to jazz, being potty about his grown-up children and trying to be a conscientious President of the Writers' Guild.

HARVEY TAYLOR was born in Newcastle and worked for many years before attending Newcastle Polytechnic as a mature student. He is a keen follower of the North-East sporting scene and a long-suffering supporter in the Gallowgate End. He is now completing his researches into the history of popular recreation at the University of Lancaster.

BILL WILLIAMSON was born in his grandparents' colliery terrace in Throckley. Educated at Lemington Grammar School, he went on to study sociology at Regent Street Polytechnic and later at the University of Durham. He is now Director of Adult and Continuing Education at Durham. Married with two children, he has spent his working life in the North-East and has written publications on education, popular culture and postwar social change. An optimist by nature, he turns to Sid Chaplin, R. H. Tawney and Raymond Williams in those moments when his optimism falters.

PAUL YOUNGER was born in 1962 at Hebburn Quay. His father was an electrical welder and his mother worked as a manager and a clerical worker. She was and still is a marvellous soprano. After Catholic schools in Jarrow and Hebburn, he read geology at Newcastle University and was a Harkness Fellow at Oklahoma State University. Married with one son, his interests are mountaineering, music (singing, songwriting, guitar, mandolin, banjo, whistle, Northumbrian pipes), writing bits and pieces, and talking politics and sport. The Younger family is now in Bolivia, where Paul is working as hydrogeologist on the Village Water Supply Project.

Guide to Further Reading

This guide is not meant to be a full scholarly bibliography on the region; rather, it is designed for the interested reader who may wish to pursue some of themes in this volume by looking at what is available in local libraries and bookshops. Those of a more scholarly disposition may be directed to A. Potts and E. R. Jones, *Northern Labour History. A Bibliography* (1981); D. J. Rowe, *Northern Business Histories. A Bibliography* 1979) and the annual Bulletins of the *North-East Labour History Society*, now in its twenty-seventh year. *The Northern Economic Review* is a useful starting point for the contemporary regional economy.

A distinguished American scholar, reviewing the *New Cambridge Social History*, vol. I *The Regions*, described the North-East as a 'strangely unknown area'. Strange indeed for an area that has as much claim as Lancashire to the title 'the cradle of the Industrial Revolution'. Generally, the region has not been well served by its historians. Norman McCord's *North-East England, The Region's Development 1760–1960* (1979) is a convenient starting point for a historical survey of the modern period. J. W. House, *The North-East* (1969), is a useful guide to the region's historical geography. H. A. Mess, *Industrial Tyneside: A Social Survey* (1928), is a stark portrait of local life at the beginning of the slump. Housing conditions, unemployment and disease, particularly TB, are sombrely explored in this period classic of social science. A fuller survey of housing is to be found in B. Lancaster (ed.) *Working-Class Housing on Tyneside* (1992).

Mining is one aspect of the region's past that has received copious scholarly attention. R. Colls, *The Pitmen of the Northern Coalfield* (1987) and *The Collier's Rant* (1977), offers the fullest modern account of the industry and its social context during the nineteenth century. We recommend also R. Moore, *Pit-Men, Preachers and Politics* (1974) and B. Williamson, *Class, Culture and Community* (1982). R. Fynes, *The Miners of Northumberland and Durham: A History of their Social and Political Progress* (1873, reprinted 1971), is a fascinating account of life in the early days of the coalfield. R. Challinor and B. Ripley, *The Miners' Association: A Trade Union in the Age of Chartists* (1968, 1990), is a useful account of the early heroic period of miners' trade unionism. J. Wilson, *A History of the Durham Miners' Association*, (1907), is an early narrative of the union in County Durham that needs to be read in conjunction with Sidney Webb, *The Story of the Durham Miners* (1921) and W. A. Garside, *The Durham Miners 1919–1960* (1971).

Sadly, local shipbuilding has not enjoyed such scholarly treatment – a curious neglect for a major regional industry that was for much of the modern period the world's largest producer of shipping tonnage. *A Century of Service to Engineering and Shipbuilding. A Centenary History of the North-East Coast Institution of Engineers and Shipbuilders, 1884–1984* (1984), by J. F. Clarke, is the best starting point into a thin literature. Tom Pickard's *We Make Ships* (1980) is a hard-hitting account of life inside the Sunderland yards during the last days of the industry – to be read alongside Ellen Wilkinson's story of Jarrow in the 1930s, *The Town That Was Murdered* (1939).

Railways, on the other hand, have been well served by enthusiastic specialist publishers producing for an equally enthusiastic readership. While one of the editors of this volume confesses that he was a former train-spotter and wasted part of his boyhood on the slaughterhouse wall overlooking Central Station, his desire to cite obscure references on Blaydon and Heaton Sheds has been firmly curtailed. The editors have taken the liberty to assume that those interested in local railway history are well aware of what is on offer in local libraries and bookshops. Those wanting a general introduction are advised to look at L. T. C. Rolt's *George and Robert Stephenson* (1978), which is still available in paperback. There are numerous company histories of individual firms available in the major local libraries, and those interested in such scholarship are advised of the recent publication of K. Warren's substantial *Armstrong's of Elswick* (1989).

Moving away from economic and industrial history, some readers may be interested in some of the broader themes of this book. The idea of the 'region' is, of course, central to all of the chapters. Those who have a taste for studying the concepts of 'community', 'regions' and 'nation' will find stimulating and provocative discussions is the following works – without whose help parts of this book could not have even been contemplated: B. Anderson, *Imagined Communities* (1983); R. Colls and P. Dodd (eds), *Englishness. Politics and Culture 1880–1920* (1986); and P. Joyce, *Visions of the People* (1991). Professor C. B. Fawcett was an early advocate of the 'North's' distinct identity, and his *Provinces of England. A Study of some Geographical Aspects of Devolution* (1919), can still be fruitfully read, particularly in conjunction with Anderson's grand theory. D. Massey's *Spacial Divisions of Labour* (1984) is a stimulating essay in Marxist geography which

GEORDIES

connects with some of the important themes in this volume. A sense of the early, inchoate period is to be gained from, in order, M. Bonney, *Lordship and the Urban Community. Durham and its Overlords 1250–1540* (1990); S. J. Watts and Susan J. Watts, *From Border to Middle Shire. Northumberland 1586–1625* (1975); and Ralph Robson, *The English Highland Clans* (1989). A fine, original history of the early modern period is provided by D. Levine and K. Wrightson, *The Making of an Industrial Society. Whickham 1560–1765* (1991) – where the authors say, revealingly, 'we wanted to fill a blank space on the historical map'. The variegated efforts of planners also need to be noted. HMSO, *An Industrial Survey of the North-East Coast Area* (1932), provided much of the raw data that fed into subsequent plans. W. A. Geenty's *County Development Plan* (1951) for Durham has gained a notoriety similar to that usually accorded to W. Burns, *Newcastle: A Study of Replanning Newcastle upon Tyne* (1967). A way into civic history is provided by S. Middlebrook, *Newcastle Upon Tyne. Its Growth and Achievement* (1950), and G. Milburn and S. Miller, *Sunderland. River, Town and People* (1988). D. J. Rowe's essay, *The North-East*, in the *Cambridge Social History of Britain*, ed. F. M. L. Thompson, vol. I (1990), is informative on quantitative data relating to the economy and population, but offers little insight into other areas of regional life. Indeed, Rowe dismisses local culture as 'a well nurtured myth'. Finally, on the subject of regionalism, Tyne and Wear 2000, *A Regional Government for the North-East of England* (1987), is the beginning of what could prove to be a lively discourse on the region's political future.

The ethnicity of the region is best explored from the literature of particular groups. S. F. Collins, *Coloured Minorities in Britain*, (1957), is an early study of blacks in Britain, and their relevance to the North-East area is discussed in Chapter 8 of this volume. The best recent study is N. Todd, 'Black on Tyne', in the *Bulletin of the North-East Labour History Society*, 21 (1987). The Irish community's rich local history is fully explored in the journal *Northern Catholic History*, which is taken by most of the major local libraries. T. P. McDermott's 'Irish Workers on Tyneside', in *Essays in Tyneside Labour History*, ed. N. McCord (1977), is also useful. For the Jewish settlement, try Lewis Olsover's *The Jewish Community of North-East England* (1980) and Arnold Levy's *History of the Sunderland Jewish Community* (1956). A general overview of migration into the area is provided in both House and Rowe mentioned above.

Women in the North-East, as in so many other parts of Britain, have been neglected by historians. The forthcoming works of D. Neville and E. Knox will, it is hoped, go some way towards redressing this imbalance. In the meantime, we have little apart from the vivid yet anecdotal *The Life and Times of Francie Nichol of South Shields* (1975) by J. Robinson, and maybe the fiction of Pat Barker and Catherine Cookson. Those interested in exploring local women's history are advised to consult *Wor Lass. Sources for*

Women's History in the North-East (1988), available from Tyne and Wear Archives Services.

Literature, drama and the visual arts are of vital importance to the region – as we hope this book has demonstrated. The writings of Jack Common and Sid Chaplin continue to cast a benign shadow over the local literary scene. *Kiddar's Luck*, published in 1951, is the seminal text of Geordie culture, but readers are urged to seek out Common's second novel, *The Ampersand* (1954), republished in 1975 in a double volume with *Kiddar's Luck*. Common's social and political writings can be found in *The Freedom of the Streets* (1938, 1988), *Seven Shifts* (1938, 1978) and *Revolt Against an 'Age of Plenty'*, ed. H. Beynon and C. Hutchinson. Sid Chaplin's beautifully crafted and nuanced writings are more numerous than Common's. *The Thin Seam* (1968), *The Day of the Sardine* (1961) and *The Watchers and the Watched* (1962) are a good introduction to the Chaplin canon. Sid, however, was also a prolific essayist. *The Leaping Lad* (1970), *The Smell of Sunday Dinner* (1971), *A Tree with Rosy Apples* (1972) and *In Blackberry Time* (1987) are all richly rewarding. For those with a taste for humour, a central feature of Geordie life, the work of Leonard Barras is a must. Enter his zany, surreal world of south-east Northumberland through the doors of *Bluebottles on my Marmalade* (1982), *Up the Tyne in a Flummox* (1988) and *Through My Hat* (1992).

The flowering of Geordie drama during the last two decades owes much to the influence of the late and much missed Cecil Taylor. His published plays include *North: Six plays* (1979), *Live Theatre: Four Plays* (1983), and *Good* and *A Nightingale Sang* (1990). Many readers of this book will need no introduction to the work of Alan Plater. His *Close the Coalhouse Door* (1969), with Sid Chaplin and Alex Glasgow, and *Going Home* (1990), are important works based on local life and experience. Tom Hadaway's much acclaimed television work is best approached by *Seacoal* (1986) and *In Fading Light* (1990), both available on Amber video.

The North-East is a highly photogenic region, much in vogue with film-makers and photographers. Sirkka-Liisa Konttinen's *Byker* (1983) and *Step by Step* (1989) are hard-edged, evocative portrayals of local life. C. Killip's *In Flagrante* (1988) is in a similar vein. Many readers will, however, more easily identify with the affectionate yet movingly accurate work of Jimmy Forsyth. His *Scotswood Road* (1986) is the photographic equivalent of *Kiddar's Luck*.

A similar humorous warmth is present in the work of the artist Norman Cornish. His *A Slice of Life* (1986) offers an autobiographical account of the trials and tribulations of combining painting and mining in the Durham coalfield. The Ashington group of mining artists have been well documented in William Feaver's *Pitmen Painters. The Ashington Group 1934–1984* (1988). The region also had a strong attraction for L. S. Lowry, who found the delights of Roker the perfect holiday venue. Juliet Horsley's *L. S. Lowry in the North-East* (1989) is a helpful account of Lowry's North-East connection. Any survey of the visual must include film and television. There is no substitute for watching the numerous works that have used the region for their backcloth, but some important issues concerned with class, region and film are covered with scholarly insight in Peter Stead's *Film and the Working Class* (1989).

The regional sporting scene has a justifiable national reputation. Football is without doubt the major activity. There is a plethora of books on local teams and players, but those in search of more scholarly fare should consult Tony Mason's *Association Football and English Society* (1980), which contains much valuable information on the early days of the game in the region. A. Appleton's *A Hotbed of Soccer* (1960) is an enthusiastic survey of North-East soccer. The importance of local cricket has been underlined by Durham's elevation to first-class county status, and our local athletes from Foster to Cram, have won many honours. Yet neither of these two important sports has been the subject of research. Similarly, rowing in the region was long overlooked, and this has only recently been amended with the publication of David Clasper's book on his illustrious ancestor, *Harry Clasper, Hero of the North* (1990).

An interesting sector of the literature on the region that deserves separate treatment is that produced by commentators from elsewhere. Ever since Dr Johnson made his disparaging remarks on Gateshead, writers have found rich pickings in the area. Yevgeny Zamyatin, the Russian novelist, lived and worked in Newcastle during the First World War. His novel *Islanders* (1984) is both a humorous portrayal of Jesmond early this century and the first instalment of his quest to write the twentieth century's first dystopian novel, *We*. Graham Turner's *The North Country* (1967) is a somewhat jaundiced exploration of regional stereotypes. A more endearing perspective is provided by John Ardagh in his *Tale of Five Cities: Life in Provincial Europe* (1979), where Newcastle emerges as the clear winner over the other European cities on his itinerary. A radically different account is provided by J. B. Priestley in his *English Journey* (1934, 1977), a famous book that continues the Johnson tradition of dismissing the region with well-turned pejoratives.

To conclude this survey, we need to return to the centre. Newcastle has produced its fair share of kitsch and nostalgia. Those who desire a more serious urban theme, however, are urged to consult the following texts. Both Patrick Wright, *On Living in an Old Country* (1985) and Robert Hewison, *The Heritage Industry* (1987), provide arguments on the relationship between past, present and the trivialisation of heritage. F. Bianchi et al., *City Centres, City Cultures* (1988), offers a prospect of city life reinvigorated through the medium of art in its many forms. The shopping phenomenon in Newcastle is briefly discussed in C. Gardner and J. Sheppard, *Consuming Passion* (1989), and is compared to the national picture. M. Barke and R. J. Buswell (eds), *Newcastle's Changing Map* (1992), is a scholarly guide to the geography of the city. The architecture of the city is lovingly portrayed in Bruce Allsopp's *Historic Architecture of Newcastle upon Tyne* (1977). But now we come to the streets, and the texts run out. May we recommend that you join the *flâneurs* and study the botany of the asphalt?

Robert Colls and Bill Lancaster

Index